Rethinking Children and Families

The Relationship between Childhood, Families and the State

Nick Frost

New Childhoods

continuum

Continuum International Publishing Group

The Tower Building
11 York Road
London SE1 7NX

80 Maiden Lane
Suite 704
New York, NY 10038

www.continuumbooks.com

© Nick Frost 2011

British Library Cataloguing-in-Publication Data
A catalogue record for this book is available from the British Library.

ISBN: 978-1-8470-6080-8 (paperback)
978-1-4411-6292-2 (hardback)

Library of Congress Cataloging-in-Publication Data
Frost, Nick, 1953–
Rethinking children and families : the relationship between childhood, families and the state/Nick Frost.
    p. cm.
Includes bibliographical references and index.
ISBN: 978-1-84706-080-8 (pbk.) — ISBN 978-1-4411-6292-2 (hardback)
1. Childhood. 2. Families. 3. State, The. I. Title.

HQ767.9.F765 2011
306.85—dc22   2010023571

Typeset by Newgen Imaging Systems Pvt Ltd, Chennai, India
Printed and bound in India by Replika Press Pvt Ltd

This book is dedicated to Lily and Alice.

Contents

List of Illustrations

Figures

Tables

Acknowledgements

I would like to thank the Series Editor, Phil Jones, for the original idea and his support throughout. Thanks to Nigel Parton, with whom I discussed the broad outline of the book, his ideas on the issues and who pointed me in the direction of the Dencik framework. Many thanks to Mike Stein, Sue Mills and Andy Lloyd for exploring many of the ideas in the book with me – usually over a curry.

Many thanks to Pam Irwin for her support with typing and layout. Thanks also to Sue Rooke for designing Figure 1.1.

Introduction to New Childhoods series

The amount of current attention given to children and to childhood is unprecedented. Recent years have seen the agreement of new international conventions, national bodies established, and waves of regional and local initiatives all concerning children.

This rapid pace has been set by many things. Demand from children themselves, from adults working with children, from governments and global bodies, new ideas and raw needs: all are fuelling change. Within and, often, leading the movement is research. From the work of multinational corporations designed to reach into the minds of children and the pockets of parents, through to charity driven initiatives aiming to challenge the forces that situate children in extreme poverty, a massive amount of energy is expended in research relating to children and their lives. Research can be seen as original investigation undertaken in order to gain knowledge and understanding through a systematic and rigorous process of critical enquiry examining 'even the most commonplace assumption' (Kellett, 2005, 9). This attention is not all benign. As Kellett has pointed out, the findings can be used by the media to saturate and accost, rather than support, under-12s who are seen as 'obese', for example, or to stigmatize young people by the use of statistics. However, research can also play a role in investigating, enquiring, communicating and understanding for the benefit of children and young people. Recent years have seen innovations in the focus of research, as political moves that challenge the ways in which children have been silenced and excluded result in previously unseen pictures of children's experiences of poverty, family life or community. The attitudes, opinions and lived experiences of children are being given air, and one of the themes within the 'New Childhoods' series concerns the opportunities and challenges this is creating. As this book will reveal, research is being used to set new agendas, to challenge ways of living and working that oppress, harm or limit children. It is also being used to test preconceptions and long held beliefs about children's lived experiences. In addition to the focus of research, innovations are being made in the way research is conceived and carried out. Its role in children's lives is changing. In the past much research treated children as objects, research was done on them, with the agenda and framework set purely by adults. New work is emerging where children create the way research is conceived and carried out. Children act as researchers, researchers work with questions formulated by children or work with children.

This series aims to offer access to some of the challenges, discoveries and work-in-progress of contemporary research. The term child and childhood is used within the series in line with Article 1 of the United Nations Convention on the Rights of the Child which defines 'children' as persons up to the age of 18. The books offer opportunities to engage with emerging ideas, questions and practices. They will help those studying childhood, or living and working with children to become familiar with challenging work, to engage with findings and to reflect on their own ideas, experiences and ways of working.

Phil Jones
Leeds University

Part 1
Debates, Dilemmas and Challenges: The Background to Relations between Childhood, Families and the State

Introduction

Introduction and key questions

This book aims to explore the complex nature of the relationship between childhood, families and the State. The main focus of the book is on how these three social phenomena are constructed, how they interact with each other and how a wide range of research, theory and scholarship can inform our views and policy and practice with children. The primary purpose of the book is to assist the reader in being able to reflect on how complex these relationships are and how we should be wary of simplistic explanations – and indeed easy solutions – to some of the dilemmas we explore here. We will see that many of the issues explored are hotly contested – in both academic and popular discourse. The main thrust of the book – and indeed the series of which it forms part – is that we need to transform our views of childhood and the way that official organizations, families and society more broadly relate to them.

In exploring these controversial debates we will be drawing on a wide range of research, scholarly writing and official documentation. The issues discussed here will hopefully have a wide resonance: the debates are very much in the public arena – watching the evening television news, or picking up a popular newspaper, on just about any day, will reveal a controversy about childhood, young people or the family. These debates also matter in our everyday life – they are about how we actually live our personal lives and how we relate to those we live with and care for (Williams, 2004).

The issues covered in this book are also important for the wide range of professionals who work with children and their families – it is mainly with these professionals and the students, who will become the professionals of the future, in mind that this book has been written.

The book has the overall aim of attempting to explore the following questions:

(a) What is the relationship between childhood, families and the State?
(b) How is this relationship changing and how can research inform us about these relationships?
(c) Why is it important to understand these relationships?
(d) How can these relationships be rethought and reinvented?

It is hoped that by the end of the book these questions have been illuminated – but the book does not pretend to provide any easy answers. What we will see is the emergence of childhood – an emergence from the shadows of history and from being treated as objects of research, to being increasingly central to social and historical research.

We will also see how childhood has become a central concern of State policies and political debates.

While the meaning of each of our main concepts – childhood, families and the State – may at first seem 'obvious' each of the three concepts are in fact deeply problematic and challenging. In this Introduction we will consider each concept in turn and thus lay the foundations on which the rest of the book aims to build.

This Introduction aims to address the following questions:

How can we define childhood, families and the State?
Why does the subject matter of this book matter?
How do childhood, the families and the State relate to each other?
What is power and why does it matter?

How can we define childhood, families and the State?

Childhood is a complex concept as it varies significantly across time (Ariès, 1979), across space/place (UNICEF, 2007) and within the same society (Bradshaw, 2002). Experiences of childhood are profoundly affected by factors such as ethnicity, class, gender and disability. Thus when we use a seemingly straight forward word like 'childhood' the stance taken in this book is that this essentially acts as a shorthand form that disguises a complex series of profoundly different life experiences and meanings. As the historian Hugh Cunningham has explained we need to distinguish

between children as human beings and childhood as a shifting set of ideas. (1995, 1)

This book, consistently with the rest of the series, utilizes:

The terms 'child' and 'childhood'…in line with Article 1 of the United Nations Convention on the Rights of the Child which defines 'children' as persons up to the age of 18. (Jones, 2009, 2)

This form of expression avoids the clumsy, if perhaps more accurate formulation, of 'children and young people'.

Families vary in a similar manner as childhood – that is historically, geographically and socially. Families can have a range of different structures – a two parent family, a one parent family, a polygamous family, or an extended family, for example – all of which are very different in the way that they exist and practice as a family. Thus once again when we speak of 'the family' we can be referring to very diverse structures and profoundly contrasting lived experiences.

The third concern of this book – the State – is also a complex idea. The State is a complicated amalgam of local, regional and national structures, which may coalesce into a coherent whole (such as the totalitarian State), or more usually form a diverse and sometimes contradictory whole (dispersed forms of government, such as devolution).

The relation between the State and the child has varied historically. In the sixteenth century State law had little to say about the child, and it would have been difficult to identify any State institutions specifically aimed at the child, until some hospitals and orphanages began to emerge in the sixteenth century (Frost et al., 1999). A fundamental shift can be seen in the second half of the nineteenth century which saw the passage of many child-orientated laws, the founding of State institutions designed to provide for children and the growth of child welfare philanthropic organizations (Hendrick, 2003). The State may be more or less interventionist in relation to childhood and different State formations can take varying policy approaches to childhood. The role of the State, and the impact of this on childhood, will form a central connecting theme of this book.

We can already see that in this book we are addressing what can be seen as a complex triangle of relationships – the key focus of the book is to consider how childhood exists in relation to families and in relation to the State. The book aims to understand these relationships and to make them both more transparent and understandable. For people studying these topics, and also for those working with children and their families, this understanding is crucial in how they actually work with children and families.

Why does the subject matter of this book matter?

As well as being important for students and professionals, the issues considered in this book are also important for society more widely. We have all been children, we have diverse experiences of childhood and families and we all exist in some sort of relationship with the State and its agents.

The importance of these issues can be seen almost everyday when we pick up a newspaper and read about an abused child, a teenage 'gang' member or an 'angelic' child who has been the victim of a crime. When we read about childhood, particularly about childhood adversity, it may well resonate with our own childhood experiences. We may have childhood memories of being abused, or of losing a parent, or perhaps of feeling abandoned and alone. As a result any study of childhood cannot pretend to view childhood as something distant and about which we are detached and dispassionate.

Our understanding of childhood also matters in terms of how we as adults relate to children, not only in official settings such as schools and hospitals, but also in everyday life in the streets and shopping centres, as well as within our own household settings.

How do childhood, families and the State relate to each other?

As the Danish sociologist Lars Dencik (1989) has pointed out, in the writings of traditional sociologists of the family, children were subsumed as part of the family. Dencik suggests instead that this is better conceived as the triangular relationship that underpins this book – the relationship between the State, parents and children. There are interactions and power relations between all three – all three help to shape and influence the other, albeit in an uneven manner. This triangular formulation is important as it sees children as potentially having interests and voices separate to, and independent of, those of their parents or carers. We have utilized the basics of this approach, albeit slightly reformulated, to underpin this book.

The series of books of which this is one aims to explore and develop the active voice of children. The series aims to analyse and explain new developments in thinking, research and practice with children. It has indeed been one of the main tenets of the 'new sociology of childhood' (James et al., 1998) to give an independent and active voice to children. As we have seen classical sociology and social policy have traditionally seen children and parents forming a whole – 'the family'– thus often having the effect of silencing the voice of children. Children being seen as simply part of a family, as the property of their parents, can still be found in some policy discussions – for example when politicians speak about 'parental choice' in relation to school preference. Approaches such as this tend to contribute to making the voices of children hidden and silent. Historically this has often been the experience of children – think, for example, of the thousands of children abused by Catholic priests in the Republic of Ireland during the twentieth century whose voices have only recently been heard.

One aim of the book is to explore how these new ideas about children can have a real impact on their lives. Part of this task is to understand how children can have interests that may differ from those of both their parents and of the State, and how their interests can be given a voice.

What is power and why does it matter?

At the centre of the relationships we explore in this book sits the exercise of power and its unequal deployment.

The State exercises power over adults through forms of governance, regulation and law. In democratic states adults also exercise some power over the State – through the ballot box and, where necessary, through recourse to legal remedies. Sometimes adults may resort to extralegal methods such as protest or revolution if the State seems to exercise illegitimate power.

The State exercises considerable power over children, as we will see throughout this book. Children have little redress except through acts of resistance (explored later in this book) and occasionally through the courts.

Adults exercise power over children – through the deployment of resources, through physical strength and punishment and through emotional power. This is mainly a one-sided-exercise form of power, with children again occasionally having recourse to the courts and trivial forms of power such as that identified by market researchers as 'pester power'.

This book argues that the exercise of power lies at the heart of the triangular relationship, which is illustrated in Figure1.1. To reinvent childhood will require massive changes in the way that power is deployed, in particular the deployment of power by the State and also by parents and carers.

The structure of the book

Having set the scene we will now move on, in Part 2 of this book, to explore each element of our triangular relationship and how power is exercised between the State, families and childhood.

In Chapter 2 we explore the social construction of childhood and demonstrate how the study of history can contribute to our contemporary understanding of childhood. Having attempted to achieve this goal the chapter moves on to explore how

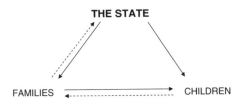

Figure 1.1 The triangular relationship (adapted from Dencik, 1989)
——— = Strong influence
------- = Weaker influence

childhood is perceived, and why this matters, and then utilizes research to explore some modern experiences of childhood.

Chapter 3 explores families, family practices and how household life has an impact on childhood. A wide range of theoretical explanations of family life are outlined and analysed. The chapter aims to explore what has been identified as 'the war over the family' (Berger and Berger, 1983).

Chapter 4 examines the third element of the triangular relationship – the State. The chapter examines a number of research studies that help us understand exactly how the State relates to the family and what happens when the State intervenes in households.

Part 1 of the book will have explored each element of the triangular relationship that lies at the heart of the book.

Part 2 of the book then outlines the implications for children's lives – analysing the connections between research, theory and the reality of life for children worldwide.

Chapter 5 examines what it is like being a child in the modern world and the impact that the State can have on this experience. A detailed case study is provided – exploring the English State's policy known as Every Child Matters. The impact the different forms of the State including liberal democratic forms and more authoritarian forms of the State can have on the everyday lived experience of children is discussed.

Chapter 6 explores the experience of being a child in the contemporary family. We see how children live in and help to construct families and households. We see how children have been treated as objects, as well as how they can be constructed as active subjects having a real impact on building family life.

Chapter 7 provides a particular focus which helps to illuminate the triangular relationship between children, families and the State. This focus explores the experiences of children who live in State care – the children who have the most direct relationship with the State, and whose lives are most dependent on how the State operates.

Chapter 8 attempts to bring together the arguments of the book and explore the possible implications of the material explored for how relations between childhood, families and the State can be reinvented to create a world where children are active subjects and less vulnerable to the abuse of adult power.

The following key themes will emerge throughout the book:

- The main relationships explored in this book are complex and challenging.
- Childhood has emerged from being hidden and silenced in recent decades.
- Childhood tends to be seen in opposing terms, such as angels/devils in a way that is unhelpful.
- The way that childhood is conceptualized has to be rethought and reinvented
- The role of the State is fundamental and indispensable to understanding childhood

Part 2
An Interdisciplinary Overview of Recent Research and Scholarship

What is Childhood?

Chapter Outline

Introduction and key questions

This chapter will explore research that has a primary focus on childhood – although all of the research explored will also have relevance to debates about families and the State. We will draw initially on historical research which is particularly informative in terms of understanding the social construction of childhood. We will then go on to examine contemporary research on children, including how children are perceived and constructed by dominant social forces. All the research will help us think about how childhood is socially constructed – that is how it varies across time and space according to the social forces which combine to form different experiences of childhood (see Jenks, 1996).

How can history help us understand childhood?

Relatively little material was produced about the history of children and childhood until the 1960s – indeed children were often absent, invisible and without a voice in historical studies. A new era, with a stronger focus on the history of childhood, began in 1960 the French historian, Philippe Ariès, published his book *L'Enfant et la vie familiale sous l'Ancien Regime*, translated into English as *Centuries of Childhood* (originally in 1962). This is probably the most high profile book written about the history of childhood – and certainly the most controversial. Almost every book written since about the history of childhood commences with a debate about Ariès' views – with many authors wanting to make it clear that they disagree with aspects of Ariès argument (see Pollock, 1983, De Mause, 1976 and Cunningham, 1995, for example). The box below outlines the key arguments made by Ariès, and we then go on to give a voice to just one of his many critics – Linda Pollock.

Example of research – discovering childhood?

Philippe Ariès' research study, 'Centuries of Childhood', was groundbreaking at the time it was published and helped to change the way we think about childhood.

Ariès' main proposal is that the concept of childhood, as we understand it, did not exist in the tenth century and was not formed until the sixteenth and seventeenth centuries and, therefore, that childhood is a relatively recent concept. There was Ariès states, in one of his most often quoted statements, 'no place for childhood in the mediaeval world' (1979, 31).

The main research materials utilized by Ariès are artistic portrayals of childhood. He argues that the realistic portrayals of childhood found in Greek art had disappeared by the Roman period and did not effectively reappear during the Middle Ages. It was not until the thirteenth century that pictures of children began to emerge and these were chiefly confined to representations of Jesus. When children did appear in paintings and other art forms they were seen as part of the adult world suggesting to Ariès that young people were absorbed into the adult world at an early age:

> It suggests too that in the realm of real life, and not simply in that of aesthetic transposition, childhood was a period which passed quickly and which was just as quickly forgotten. (1979, 32)

Ariès sees the likelihood of early childhood death as one explanation and he quotes parents expressing lack of regret at the passing of their children. It was only in the

⇨

---

sixteenth century that the dead child began to appear in portraits:

> the appearance of the dead child in the sixteenth century...marked a very important moment in the history of feelings. (1979, 38)

Eventually, Ariès points out, children began to appear in their own portraits:

> henceforth he would be depicted by himself and for himself: this was the great novelty of the seventeenth century. (1979, 40)

Another research source utilized by Ariès is fashion and childhood dress. According to his findings childhood dress during the mediaeval period could not be differentiated from that of adults:

> as soon as the child abandoned his swaddling – band...he was dressed just like other men and women of his class. (1979, 48)

The similarity of adult and childhood dress only began to change in the seventeenth century:

> the adoption of a special childhood costume , which became generalized throughout the upper classes as from the end of the sixteenth century, marked a very important date in the formation of the idea of childhood. (1979, 55)

According to Ariès, boys and girls were dressed alike until they were about five; but in sixteenth century the idea of childhood dress began to emerge first for boys and later for girls:

> if we confine our attention to the evidence afforded by dress, we must con-clude that the particularization of children was limited for a long time to boys. What is certain is that it occurred solely in the middle class or aristocratic fam-ilies. (1979, 59)

Ariès goes on to explore children's games and the transitions into the adult world largely drawing on Heroard's diary, the doctor of Louis XIII, when Louis was a child. Ariès argues that Louis was quickly absorbed into the adult world. Early in his life, when he was 17 months of age, he became involved in playing the violin, there is evidence of sexual banter from two years upwards and, by the age of seven, he was absorbed into the adult world, including being involved in gambling, riding, hunting and drinking. Louis XIII then went on to be married at the age of 14.

Ariès builds on this evidence to conclude the first part of his book by stating that

> in medieval society the idea of childhood did not exist: this is not to suggest that children were neglected, forsaken or despised. The idea of childhood is not to be confused with affection for children: it corresponds to an awareness of the particular nature of childhood, that particular nature which distin-guishes the child from the adult...in mediaeval society, this awareness was lacking (1979, 125)

⇨

Ariès concludes that childhood began to emerge in the fourteenth century and was established during the sixteenth- and seventeenth centuries. Childhood, according to Ariès, emerged in two main arenas – the family and the school.

> In the family the child emerged as an object of sweetness, and of being cared for and 'coddled'. Ariès argues that by the mid eighteenth century, 'the child has taken a central place in the family'. (1979, 130)

Childhood also emerged as a social space which churchmen and moralists wanted to influence and shape through schooling:

> A new moral concept was to distinguish the child, or at least the schoolboy, and set him apart: the concept of the well-bred child. It scarcely existed in the sixteenth century. We know it was the product of the reforming opinions of an elite of thinkers and moralists who occupied high positions in church or state. (1979, 315)

This quotation provides, even today, an important formulation which we return to later in this book.

Reflections on the research

This is important and groundbreaking research which is worthy of reflection and analysis. Ariès' proposition that childhood was discovered set the agenda for the history of childhood, and provides valuable insights into the social construction of childhood.

Activity 1

Reflect on the research sources that Ariès utilized to undertake his research. How reliable are these sources? What sources could we use today if we were undertaking a modern history of childhood?

Activity 2

Are you convinced by Ariès' core idea that childhood was 'discovered'?

We have devoted some considerable space to the work of Ariès as it sets down a marker for research on the history of childhood and what we mean by social construction. His research was groundbreaking and his contention that childhood was 'discovered' rather than 'natural' was quite breathtaking at the time in its' implications. But as is often the case with research other researchers differ from the main findings of Ariès. One of his primary critics is another historian, Linda Pollock. She differs profoundly from Ariès and uses detailed and extensive studies of diaries to establish her case.

Example of research – diaries as a research tool

The historical researcher Linda Pollock has utilized extensive diary-based research to challenge the work of Ariès. Pollock argues that her evidence suggests that affection between parents and children has been relatively constant over the past five centuries, hence she proposes what we might characterize as a 'continuity' position. This contrasts with the 'change' school of Ariès among many other historians.

Pollock identifies three major strands of the 'change' school that she wishes to use her diary research to challenge. These are

1. the 'Ariès thesis' that there was no concept of childhood during the medieval period;
2. that there was a lack of affection in parent-child relationships;
3. that until the eighteenth century and again in the nineteenth century children were abused and exploited.

Pollock suggests that her historical diary-based evidence challenges each of these three propositions. She also argues that they reflect a key error in the methods that the historians have utilized, namely that

> if a past society did not possess the contemporary Western Concept of childhood then that society had no such concept. (1983, 263)

In her criticism of the advocates of the three proposals Linda Pollock makes the following arguments against other researchers:

- that their historical evidence has been used superficially
- that some of their historical research has been poor
- that the same evidence has been used to support contradictory positions.

Pollock suggests, for example, that because most historians of childhood have concentrated on the punishment of children, this has over-emphasized the presence of abuse. Edward Shorter, for example, argues that

> children were brutalised by the daily routines of life as much by the savage outbursts of parental rage. (1976, 170)

Pollock responds that this focus on the negative aspects of parent – child interactions means that the general contexts of children's lives have been under-explored by historians of childhood.

Through the use of extensive diary evidence Pollock is able to deduce the following points:

- there is a close congruity between accounts given by parents and children
- that sixteenth-century diarists did indeed have a concept of childhood
- that there are many examples of parent child affection present in the diaries.

As a consequence of her extensive research into diaries she argues that

> there have been very few changes in parental care and child life from the sixteenth to the nineteenth century in the home. (1983, 268)

⇨

Pollock's intensive and extensive research detects many examples of affection between parents and children and a more limited degree of cruelty than is normally suggested. She turns the argument of many in the 'change school' on its head by arguing that the existence of newspaper reports of child abuse in the early nineteenth century indicates that such incidents

> were regarded as 'inhuman' aberrations from the norm rather than typical. This contradicts the arguments of many historians that adults were indifferent to children. (1983, 95)

The following quote from one of Pollock's diaries demonstrates that there was evidence of very real affection:

> Newcome (1627–95) was clearly devoted to his offspring. From the information in his diary, he sees his role as helping them throughout their lives. His sons wrote of him as a 'loving and faithfull [*sic*] father to his children' and also a 'revered and dear father...whose authority we revered, and whose indulgent care over us was one of our greatest supports'. (1983, 265)

Pollock provides many similar examples. She detects some changes in attitude to childhood over the centuries but argues that these are, 'very minor compared with the image of continuity provided by the sources' (1983, 269).

In order to place her research evidence in a theoretical framework Pollock utilizes 'socio-biology' to argue that there has always been a natural, biological basis to affection between parents and their children.

Reflections on the research

Pollock expresses some profound differences with the work of Ariès that we examined in the previous research box. Pollock is keen to argue for continuity in the experience of childhood – whereas Ariès was keen to emphasis change and discontinuity.

Activity one

Pollock largely utilized diaries to undertake her research. How reliable are diaries as a tool for understanding childhood?

Activity two

Are you convinced by Pollock's core idea that parents have always loved their children, and that this is underpinned by a strong biological link? Can you think of any examples that may disprove Pollock's theory?

Thus we commence our discussion of the history and social construction of childhood by unearthing a major dispute amongst researchers. Conflict and difference is a major theme of thinking and research about children and families – later in the book we will unearth many other fundamental disputes between researchers and scholars about how we can understand childhood and families.

Stephanie Coontz helpfully summarizes the disputes between historians as follows:

> Some historians argued that, in general, parents were uncaring and marriages were loveless before the advent of 'affective individualism'. Closer historical examination revealed that such generalisations rested on ethnocentric mis-readings of evidence. This led to a spate of studies attempting to establish continuity of families' ties and emotions. (2000, 284)

Here Coontz argues that 'ethnocentrism', in other words, that researchers sometimes privilege their own world view, is the key to the dispute. Other critics have focused more how research evidence is utilized. What matters most for this book is to reflect on how there are often disputes about issues that have an impact on our understanding of childhood and families.

It is a major, and perhaps impossible, challenge for historians to uncover diverse childhoods: not least because it tends to be privileged and literate children who tend to be more visible to the gaze of the historian.

Thus far in this chapter we have explored historical perspectives on childhood and a theoretical study which represent a major breakthrough in the study of childhood. We complete the chapter by examining perceptions of children and end with a research example which helps to illustrate how children experience life today.

How is childhood perceived?

As we have already argued childhood is a diverse and multifaceted phenomenon that is difficult and complex to analyse. In this section we will explore how childhood is perceived by the media and in popular discourse, and then assess the impact that this has on political initiatives around childhood.

The childhood researcher, Christopher Jenks, has argued that children are seen using two major divisions – as 'little angels' or 'little devils'. While Jenks is a sociologist it can be noted that a similar argument has been made drawing largely on literary sources by Marina Warner (1989), and also by the social historian Harry Hendrick (2003). The social geographer, Gill Valentine, puts this key point as follows:

> ...contemporary parents perceive their own children to be innocent and vulnerable (angels) whilst simultaneously representing other people's children as out of control in public space and a threat to moral order (devils). (1996, 581–582)

We will move on to explore how children are seen as falling into one of these two camps and then move on to why these representations might be significant in terms of State approaches to childhood.

Initially let us explore how children are seen as 'little angels'. Certainly children are viewed in this manner when they are 'victims' of crime or violence. For example, the 16 children murdered in their school in Dunblane, Scotland, in March, 1996, were described as 'little angels' (see popular press coverage of this tragic event) in the media coverage of their murders. Equally children murdered by their parents are usually portrayed in the same way. Images of 'little angels' are also used in portraits (famously in Millais' portrait of an angelic young man often used in adverts) and regularly in adverts for a wide range of products including those aimed at children, as well as other products. Underpinning these images are often unspoken ideas about childhood – that they are born innocent, are powerless and passive, and that they can be victims of adult violence and aggression.

In contrast to this view children are also seen as 'little devils'. The obvious category being children who have committed crimes – the two boys who murdered James Bulger in England provide an extreme example of this where the boys were widely portrayed as 'evil' and 'devil children'. This latter phrase being also used in 2010 to describe two boys who assaulted two others boys in Doncaster. This image of children as evil – as being uncivilized and containing evil intrinsically within them is often seen in literature – a clear example being in William Golding's novel ' Lord of the Flies', or in the film 'The Exorcist'. The author saw a recent English railway advert showing children as devils with tails and tridents , with the tag line being 'take the little devils to the seaside'.

Here we can see what sociologists refer to as 'bifurcation' – that a category can be divided into two opposing camps: in this case children are either 'little devils' or 'little angels'. This crude divide is problematic in a number of ways. First of all none of us tend to fall simply into any one category – we may be generally cheerful, but sometimes feel depressed, for example. Equally such a bifurcation tends to oversimplify change over time and in differing circumstances – we all change over time and our behaviour is largely dependent on the circumstances we find ourselves in. For example, a normally shy and introvert person may become noisy and demonstrative when part of a football crowd. Thus reducing human beings to an essential element, known in sociology as 'essentialism', is fraught with difficulties. With children this is particularly challenging as it may well be that the innocent, angelic child murdered by its father may well otherwise have gown up to be the aggressive 'hoodie' hated by the popular media.

Geoffrey Pearson undertook an influential study of how the 'respectable classes' viewed crime and morals – and often associated this with children and young people. His study illustrates the long history of how modern children have been consistently viewed as more problematic than children were 'twenty years ago'.

Example of research – understanding fear of young people and crime

Geoffrey Pearson undertook a study of how the British perceived the threat of the 'hooligan' through the late Victorian era until the time he wrote his book in the early 1980s. He finds strong continuities in the way that 'respectable people' have worried about street crime and 'hooligans' – who were usually young people. He finds that there are often fears about the current generation of young people and a longing for a golden era – that was 'twenty years ago' and which Pearson's evidence suggest never actually existed. He provides compelling evidence about how dominance views have often complained that the children of today are worse than children of the past. Some of these are contemporary but others go back many years, for example a quote from Lord Ashley in the House of Commons, 1843, who complained that, 'the morals of the children are tenfold worse than formerly' (1983, 119).

Pearson concludes:

> What this historical journey has revealed to us…is a seamless tapestry of fears and complaints about the deteriorated present; a long and connected history that makes plain the shortcomings of the more usual view of our cultural inheritance which is severely limited by its simple nostalgia for the old 'way of life'. (1983, 209)

Reflections on research

This is a groundbreaking study, that also makes interesting, and at times, amusing reading. The power of the analysis is demonstrated by the fact that the analysis still works today, even though the book was written in the 1980s.

⇨

Activity 1

Pearson argues that children are often regarded as problematic and it is felt that they are worse than children from previous decades. How do you think the contemporary media views children and young people?

Activity 2

Which current activities and interests of children are regarded as a threat in some media coverage?

Pearson has provided a very compelling history of how negative attitudes towards children and young people have often prevailed (see Scruton, 1997, for further discussion of these issues).

For a more recent example of research than Pearson's we will explore research commissioned by the children's charity Barnardo's which illustrates that these negative attitudes to young people are still with us.

Research example – feral children and out of control young people

The British charitable organization Barnardo's (2008) undertook a study of public perceptions of childhood. The polling organisation YouGov interviewed 2,021 adults. A number of statements were made and people were asked if they agreed with them.
  The findings show that

- just under half (49 per cent) of people agree that children are increasingly a danger to each other and adults;
- Forty-three per cent agree something has to be done to protect us from children;
- more than a third (35 per cent) of people agree that nowadays it feels like the streets are infested with children;
- Forty-five per cent of public agree that people refer to children as feral because they behave this way;
- nearly half of the people (49 per cent) disagree with the statement that children who get into trouble are often misunderstood and in need of professional help.

  The public's intolerance is also reflected in the British Crime Survey, which indicates that the public felt young people committed up to half of all crime when in actual fact young people are responsible for only 12% of crime. (Barnardo's, 2008)

  ⇨

Barnardo's conclude, perhaps rather dramatically, that

> There is an unjustified and disturbing intolerance of children in the U.K. (Barnardo's, 2008)

Reflections on the research

This research from Barnardo's has been controversial as it provided statements – such as that about feral children – and asked respondents if they agree with them. Some critics have argued that this suggested answers to respondents (Rothwell, 2008).

Activity 1

Give an example of how modern children are regarded negatively.

Activity 2

Are British children regarded more negatively than children elsewhere in the world?

It is noteworthy that a similar point is made by the United Nations High Commission on Human Rights who argue that the United Kingdom should

> take urgent measures to address the intolerance and inappropriate characterisation of children, especially adolescents, within society, including the media. (UNHCR, 2008)

Certainly there seems to be an issue with the way that children are portrayed in the media and how this has an impact on people's perceptions of children. As Jones (2009) has argued in this series these perceptions matter as they have a real impact on law and policy:

> attitudes and large group thinking and feeling combine to create national or local government policies, laws procedures and ways of treating children. (2009, 107)

How can childhood be reinvented?

In the 1980s a number of authors made what is widely recognized as a breakthrough in our understanding of childhood – this work is often referred to as 'the new sociology of childhood'. In many ways we can compare this work to the research undertaken by Ariès – both bodies of work have contributed to new ways of thinking about childhood.

The key authors in this paradigm include Jens Qvortup, Allison James, Chris Jenks and Alan Prout – the latter three of whom often work together. One of their key books is outlined in the 'example of research' box below: other examples of their work can be found in the references. The international journal *Childhood* provides an important forum for discussing and disseminating important scholarship around the theme of the 'new sociology of childhood'. The box below provides the key features of 'new sociology of childhood'.

Example of research – a new paradigm for the sociology of childhood

During the 1990s there was a major sociological breakthrough which created a new way of researching childhood – the research example explored here summarizes this work well: *Theorising Childhood*, by James, Prout and Jenks.

They summarize their intention as follows:

> To provide an analytical framework that will act both to consolidate the now burgeoning army of childhood studies and to indicate trails and pointer s for further work in the area. (1998, 195)

They share the perspective of this book that the study of childhood is complex and challenging; they centre their work on four key dichotomies:

- Structure and agency
- Identity and difference
- Continuity and change
- Local and global (James et al., 1998, 199)

They also argue that children are understood in four key ways:

> The social structural child –
> they are part of the very constitution of social life and therefore should be understood as an integral form within every and any social system. (1998, 209)
> The minority group child –
> this mode recognizes that children are structurally differentiated within societies, and that, as such, they experience the exercise of power differently, and in particular in its institutionalized and legitimated forms. (1998, 211)
> The socially constructed child –
> there is no essential child but always one that is built up through constitutive practices, in either a string or weak sense. (1998, 212)
> The tribal child –

⇨

inhabits a social category, that is essence, their own. Their culture is to be regarded as the self-maintaining system of signs, symbols and rituals that prescribes the whole way of life of children within a particular socio historical setting. (1998, 215)

The authors conclude that they hope they have provided

a platform for future research initiatives and modes of inquiry that might usefully stem from the new social studies of childhood, to combine in the endeavour that is *theorizing childhood*. (1998, 218)

Reflections on the research

The 'new sociology of childhood' produced a new way of thinking about childhood. It recognized children as real, actual, existing people in their own right – not as 'future' or 'partly formed' human beings.

Activity One

It is widely thought that the 'new sociology of childhood' helped to produce a new way of thinking about children. Can you outline how this is the case?

Activity Two

If you were undertaking some research about an aspect of contemporary childhood using the 'new sociology of childhood' what principles, ideas and concepts could you draw on in undertaking your research?

We can see in the 'new sociology of childhood' the major challenges that childhood studies need to address:

(a) to construct childhood as an active process in which the role of children as authors of their own lives is fully recognized;
(b) to recognize the diversity of childhood as it is constructed by experiences of social divisions such as social class, disability, ethnicity and gender.

We have seen how research about childhood has unfolded, from children being invisible in scholarship, to a new paradigm that has argued for the centrality of childhood. Childhood exists in a complex relationship to families which we will go on to explore in the following chapter.

Activities

The following activities are designed to help reflect back on some of the key concerns over the chapter as a whole.

Activity 1

We have seen that there are disputes between historians who believe that the history of childhood is marked by change and discontinuity (such as Ariès) and those who place an emphasis on continuity (such as Pollock).

Reflect on your own childhood: make a list of any changes between your childhood and those of children you know today.
Think about issues such as

- play
- material goods
- travel
- school
- family structure
- punishment
- being listened to

Has childhood changed during this period? If it has what are the main drivers of this change?

Activity 2

We have seen that children are portrayed along a divide as 'little angels' or as 'little devils'. Keep a log, say for the next week, of images you see of children on TV, adverts or in the press. What themes emerge from your observations?

Activity 3

One of the main tenets of the 'new sociology of childhood' is that childhood is socially constructed. We can argue that this means childhood varies according to time (when the child existed), place (where the child existed) and social divisions of childhood (the class, gender, dis/ability, ethnicity).

How convinced are you by this argument? Do you think childhood is more marked by what all children have in common?

Summary

This chapter has

- explored the groundbreaking work of Philippe Ariès on the history of childhood;
- examined how some historians, specifically Linda Pollock, have used further research to outline their disagreements with Ariès;

- outlined a recent approach to childhood, 'the new sociology of childhood';
- explored how this can be applied to researching the contemporary lives of children.

Further reading

Cunningham, H. (1995) *Children and Childhood in Western Society since 1500.* London: Longman

This book provides an excellent and accessible summary of the history of childhood and the disputes between historians that have been touched upon in this chapter.

Jenks, C. (1996) *Childhood.* London: Routledge

This book provides a brief overview of the debates about the social construction of childhood that underpin many of the arguments explored in this book.

Postman, N. (1994) *The Disappearance of Childhood.* New York: Vintage

A classical study which explores the origins of childhood – which Postman convincingly argues relates to the introduction of the printing press. Postman also argues that the media is currently contributing to the 'disappearance of childhood'.

Smith, R. (2010) *A Universal Child?* Basingstoke: Palgrave

An excellent overview of the scholarship and theorizing about children – it also provides a clear focus on the policy and practice implications of these debates.

Research details

Discovering childhood

Philippe Ariès produced the most influential book on the history of childhood – albeit one that is often criticized by other historians and commentators. Originally written in French in 1960 the book has been reprinted many times in numerous languages. His proposition that childhood was 'discovered' provides the basis for exploring childhood as a social construction.

Ariès, P. (1979) *Centuries of Childhood.* Harmondsworth: Peregrine

Diaries as a research tool

Among the most high profile of Ariès critics, Pollock's meticulous research of diaries is impressive. Arguably her thesis is marred by an unnecessary appeal to 'socio-biology' as a theoretical base for her work.

Pollock, L. (1983) *Forgotten Children*. Cambridge: Cambridge University Press

Understanding fear of young people and crime

Geoffrey Pearson has written what is probably the classic account of the fear of crime and how this is often linked with perceptions of children. He demonstrates how people imagine that there was a 'golden age' of childhood – which always existed 20 or 30 years ago. Pearson argues that this is often a fear of modernity and new developments – citing a Victorian fear of cyclists as an example!

Pearson, G. (1983) Hooligan: *A History of Respectable Fears* London: MacMillan

Feral children and out of control young people

Barnardo's, the children's charity, undertook a controversial study of how the public perceived children. They found a widespread fear of children, linked to crime and anti-social behaviour, and found that many adults viewed children as being 'feral' and out of control.

Barnardo's (2008) *The Shame of Britain's Intolerance to Children*, Barkingside: Barnardo's

A new paradigm for the sociology of childhood

This is the key book that outlines the approach taken by what has been called 'the new sociology of childhood'. This approach sees children as real human beings in their own right – rather than as being immature, or part-formed adults. The implications for this approach, alongside the United Nations Convention on the Rights of the Child, form the basis of a new and emerging approach to researching, understanding and ultimately working with children.

James, A., Jenks, C. and Prout, A. (1998) *Theorising Childhood*. Cambridge: Polity Press

Families and Family Practices

Introduction and key questions

In the previous chapter we saw that the history of childhood is a contested field where historians often disagree with each other. We now move on to examine research about families – which, we will find, is an equally contested field of study.

The media and politicians often utilize, or perhaps exploit, research to support their particular ideas and perspectives on family life – thus the publication of official statistics are often greeted by controversy about the 'decline of the family', the 'ease of obtaining a divorce' or the 'increase in single parent families'.

In this chapter we explore why research concerned with families and household life is often contested. The following questions will be addressed in this chapter:

- How can research on the family contribute to our understanding?
- How can theory and research contribute to a contemporary view of the family?
- How can we analyse families in a way that recognizes the active role of children?

Family research and diverse perspectives on families

Carol Smart reflects on debates about the family as follows:

> Perhaps the most significant of these debates around family life have been those between (1) ideas of the demise of the extended family and the rise of the 'modern' nuclear family; (2) the decline of marriage as an economic contract and the rise of companionate relationships between spouses; (3) the changing status of childhood and the growth of child-centredness; (4) and latterly the decline of the nuclear family and the rise of fluid family practices. (Smart, 2007, 10)

It is the fourth debate that will be the focus of this chapter. We commence with examples of research from very different ideological stances and which demonstrate how family research is indeed a political minefield. Our first example comes from a researcher on the right of political thinking – a British 'think tank' known as the Institute for Economic Affairs (IEA). This research makes claims that the traditional family unit is in decline and this is a regrettable state of affairs. It is based mainly on quantitative research about what is happening in British family life.

Example of research: Broken Britain? – the declining and shattered family

Patricia Morgan argues that the traditional family unit is in decline and that this is a regrettable state of affairs. Her perspective can be contrasted with the argument made by Williams in the next 'example of research' box.

Utilizing official statistics Morgan argues that the approach taken by authors such as Williams means that

> Where the definition of family is stretched to cover any household, where any living situation and all transitional states are equally 'families', there is nothing to decline or dissolve, only movement between ever-transmuting 'family forms'. (1998, 66)

She argues that in fact people still aspire to 'family values' and that changes in household forms reflect as failure to achieve these aspirations:

> Failure to attain conventional goal, rather than the eager embrace of 'alternatives', is perhaps reflected in the way that (the number of) married couples fell…while cohabiting couples with children increased. (1998, 68)

⇨

This has gender implications:

> If men no longer have to assume parental responsibility to engage in sexual relations, the women can marry the State instead – something with greatest appeal to those whose personal economic, as well as marital options, are limited. (1998, 70)

Morgan also regrets easily access to divorce:

> Liberalised divorce certainly alters the nature of the contract it terminates. Lacking the power to bind future behaviour, the incentive to invest resources in a relationship is undermined. (1998, 72)

Morgan, using data on outcomes for children, argues that the traditional dual parent family unit promotes the best interests of children, as nothing alters:

> the *fact* that family structures may differ in the opportunities they offer to growing children...the number of children with psychosocial disorders has grown over the same time as families have increasingly fractured and fragmented...lone parenthood is the strongest socio-demographic predictor of childhood injury...children are more likely to go into care following a crisis when the family is 'reconstituting' itself. (1998, 74)

For Morgan the implications are wide-ranging:

> the obverse of family disruption and contraction tends to be low rates of participation in community activities and organisations on the part of lone mothers and single men compared to married women and fathers. (1998, 80)

She concludes:

> While the effects of family breakdown are already apparent, acceptance of the end of marriage and decline of the family is premature. The first step towards recovery is to stop describing social changes as though they were inevitable. (1998, 82)

Reflections on research

Patricia Morgan is a researcher who believes that the traditional family unit is in decline and that this is a regrettable state of affairs.

Activity 1
Morgan argues that the family is in decline. How convincing do you find the arguments that she presents?

Activity 2
Reflect on how 'social facts', for example the increase in the number of single parent families, are utilized to make value statements, for example the increase in the number of single parent families is a negative development. What processes are at work here?

In examining the influential work undertaken by Patricia Morgan we witness one school of family research that can be identified as being 'pessimistic' about developments in the modern family. This school of thought argues that recent developments in family life have been negative and are clearly undesirable. But, as we have already speculated, there is another side of the debate – what we might identify as coming from a 'progressive' or 'feminist' perspective. From these schools of research come findings and analysis that in many ways agree that the traditional family is changing rapidly, but this work has a very different tone and some sharply contrasting political and everyday implications from those argued above by Patricia Morgan.

The contrasting example comes from an Economic and Social Research Council (ESRC)-funded programme of research which is central to the concerns of this book – the project was known as CAVA (Care, Values and the Future of Welfare) and which was based at the University of Leeds, United Kingdom. The example of research box below explores the main findings of this project, as outlined by Fiona Williams (2004).

Examples of research: new ways of doing family

The CAVA research took place over five years and involved a team of eminent researchers. The work explored five central themes: life after divorce; motherhood, work and care; non-conventional partnerships; transnational kinship; and collective groups who mobilize around parenting and partnering issues.

The project utilized a range of qualitative approaches and aimed to find out 'what matters' to people. The team argue that 'we have a greater diversity of living arrangements and family forms' (2004, 11) than existed previously. To understand these changes the research team utilize

> the concept of 'family practices' which focuses on the everyday interactions with close and loved ones and moves away from the fixed boundaries of co-residence, marriage, ethnicity and obligation that once defined the…nuclear family. It registers the ways in which our networks of affection are not simply given by virtue of blood and marriage but are negotiated and shaped by us, over time and place. (2004, 17)

What defines family practices is that they are fluid and changing. Family is not seen by this school of research as a fixed and predefined social institution, rather family is what we do, or how we practise family and kinship.

Having analysed their findings the research team argue that

- the shape of commitment is changing but there is no loss of commitment (2004, 7)

⇨

- sex and living together are no longer essential bedfellows (2004, 7)
- people care in different ways (2004, 8)
- when changes conflict with values...people cope with this by weighing up how best to sustain their relationships with people who matter to them (2004, 8)
- self-help groups play an important role in communities in providing the sort of care and support that people say they want (2004, 8)
- what many people share is not an agreement on a set of abstract moral imperatives, but a moral and social weighing-up of a given situation (2004, 8)

Reflections on the research

This research is very different from that of Morgan, which we explored earlier. The research team celebrate change and the new ways we have of caring for those we look after and live with.

Activity 1
Compare and contrast the arguments of the CAVA team with those of Patricia Morgan What are the key similarities and differences?

Activity 2
Can you recognize any of the trends suggested by CAVA in your own life or in the lives of people that you know?

Thus far we have examined the findings and analysis of two diverse schools of research. We have seen that family research is notable for dispute between the research findings and analysis – just as we saw that there was a significant divergence among researchers who had focused on the history of childhood. The American researchers, Berger and Berger, entitled one of their books 'The War over the Family' (1983), in recognition of just how contested family research and politics are.

How can theory and research contribute to contemporary views of the family?

In Figure 3.1 we illustrate some of the different theoretical perspectives on families and the implications they have for children. We can see that there a number of different theories of the family.

	FUNCTIONALIST	COMMUNITARIAN	MARXIST	FAMILY PRACTICES	FEMINIST
WHAT IS THE ROLE OF THE FAMILY ?	TO PLAY THE KEY ROLE IN THE SOCIALIZATION AND UP BRINGING OF CHILDREN	TO RAISE CHILDREN IN THE BEST POSSIBLE WAY AND TO CONTRIBUTE POSITIVELY TO THE COMMUNITY	TO ENSURE THAT RULING IDEAS ARE TRANSMITTED AND THAT PRIVATE PROPERTY IS MAINTAINED	PEOPLE CREATE THEIR OWN MEANINGS FROM HOW THEY ACTUALLY LIVE	TO REPRODUCE MALE DOMIN-ATION
WHICH THEORISTS HOLD THESE POSITIONS ?	TALCOTT PARSONS FERDINAND MOUNT	AMITIA ETZIONI ANTHONY GIDDENS	FREDERIC ENGELS ELI ZARETSKY	FIONA WILLIAMS LEONORA DAVIDOFF	ANN OAKLEY JULIET MITCHELL
HOW SHOULD THE FAMILY CHANGE ?	DIVORCE SHOULD BE DIS-COURAGED THE FAMILY SHOULD BE STRENGTHENED	SOCIETY SHOULD PROMOTE THE ROLE OF THE FAMILY THERE SHOULD BE MORE EMPHASIS ON CHILD REARING	ABOLISH THE FAMILY OR THE STRENGTHS OF THE WORKING-CLASS FAMILY SHOULD BE BUILT UPON	WIDER DEFINITION OF CARE MORE FLEXIBLE LIFESTYLES	WOMEN SHOULD HAVE MORE RIGHTS OR ABOLISH THE FAMILY
WHAT DOES IT MEAN FOR CHILDREN ?	CHILDREN CAN BE EFFECTIVELY SOCIALIZED THROUGH STRONG FAMILIES	CHILDREN SHOULD BE THE CENTRAL FOCUS FOR THE FAMILY	CHILDREN ARE BROUGHT UP WITHIN RULING IDEAS AND VALUES	WIDER RELATIONSHIPS AND CARING NETWORKS TO BE TAKEN SERIOUSLY	CHILDREN, FEMALES ARE OPPRESSED BY MEN
WHAT IS THE ALTERNATIVE?	NONE – THE FAMILY IS THE CENTRAL SOCIAL INSTITUTION	MORE PUBLIC SUPPORT FOR FAMILIES / MORE RESPONSIBLE PARENTING	SOCIALIST EQUALITY / ABOLITION OF THE FAMILY	ETHIC OF CARE / FLUIDITY	MORE EQUAL FAMILIES / ABOLITION

Figure 3.1 Theories of the family – differing perspectives?

How can we make sense of all these different theories? We now move on to suggest a theoretical perspective that will help inform the rest of the book.

In order to bring together the findings from this chapter we will utilize the work of Anthony Giddens, a renowned sociologist and former Director of the London School of Economics.

Giddens argues that the changes we are experiencing over recent decades can be understood through the lens of 'globalization' and 'modernization':

> As tradition changes its role . . . new dynamics are introduced into our lives . . . where tradition has retreated, we are forced to live in a more open and reflective way. (1999, 46)

Giddens argues that these changes can be unsettling, and bring with them problems and challenges. Think, for example, about new technology – it is often embraced by younger people, while older people may, particularly at first, struggle with the new developments – be these Twitter, the smart phone or the digital book. But, Giddens argues just because these developments are complex or unsettling, it does not mean that they should be regretted. Thus Giddens argues that while family practices have changed and that these changes are unsettling for many, they should be broadly welcomed for, 'the inequality of men and women was intrinsic to the traditional family' (1999, 54).

In terms of children he reflects as follows:

> The idea of enshrining children's rights in law in historical terms is relatively recent. In pre-modern periods, as in traditional cultures today, children weren't reared for their own sake . . . one could say that children weren't recognised as individuals. It wasn't that parents didn't love their children, but they cared for them more for the contribution they made to the common economic task than for themselves. (1999, 55)

A thinker within the same tradition as Giddens, Beck Gernsheim, reflects on how complex these developments are for our understanding of the family:

> The result of all these changes is that, in politics, academic research and everyday life, it is no longer clear who or what is part of the family. The boundaries are becoming unclear, the definitions uncertain. There is a growing loss of security. (2002, 2)

Giddens writes of the 'democratic family', where women have more say and where children have a voice, which he identifies as

> a democracy of the emotions in everyday life...this applies as much in parent-child relationships as in other areas...they should assume an in principle equality...in a democracy of the emotions, children can and should be able to answer back. (1999, 63)

This is in contrast with the 'traditional family' which was dominated by the father and where women and children were subjugated, and sometimes, were the victims of sexual or physical violence. Beck Gernshiem reflects on the traditional family as follows:

> parents were supposed to ensure that children received moral instruction and were inculcated with a fear of God, obedience and work, as well as providing them with the elementary needs of food and clothing. There was also a certain degree of supervision, to guard against accidents such as drowning, and a lot of physical correction, often in the form of beating. (2002, 88)

Thus both Giddens and Beck Gernshiem argue that the modern, 'democratic family' should be welcomed as a modern and progressive space for us to live in and to construct our personal lives. It is thus important to avoid what Qvortup calls 'familiarization' which

> implies keeping children hidden in the family, inaccessible to the public gaze. For children, this can be detrimental. (2005, 10)

Giddens is often identified as a 'communitarian' – see Figure 3.1 for what this means. But there is a variation within communitarianism, with the American theorist Etzioni representing a trend which places the emphasis on responsibilities, as opposed to rights. This can be clearly seen in the following quote where Etzioni argues that

> Making a child is a moral act. Obviously it obligates the parents to the child. But it also obligates the parents to the community. (1993, 54)

There is a strong emphasis in Etzioni's work that the needs of children should be prioritized:

> parents have a moral responsibility to the community to invest themselves in the proper upbringing of their children, and communities – to enable parents to so dedicate themselves. (1993, 54)

And he also argues for gender equality in terms of child rearing:

> the issue is the dearth of parental involvement of both varieties: mothers and fathers. (1993, 55)

In some ways, unlike Giddens, Etzioni allies himself with the sorts of views we have seen the clearly right-wing thinker, Patricia Morgan, express earlier:

> there are several compelling reasons why two-parent families are the most suitable form for children. (Etzioni, 1993, 60)

Having examined these diverse perspectives on childhood and families we now move on to look at the third aspect of our triangle – the State and various agencies. In the concluding chapter we will bring together a perspective which draws together our argument and puts forward a model for rethinking childhood and families, and the role of the State in this.

Activities

The following activities are designed to help reflect back on some of the key concerns over the chapter as a whole.

Activity 1

We have seen that the family is changing and that it is more fluid and flexible than in the past. How does your family actually 'practise family'? Can you think of any factors about your family that seem specific to your family and kinship network? How many people live in 'non-conventional' situations? Is there any one counted as family who in biological terms strictly is not family?

Activity 2

We have seen how there are contrasting perspectives on the family – for example contrasting Fiona Williams and Patricia Morgan's views. Why is 'the family' politically divisive? Why is there what Berger and Berger refer to as a war over the family?

Summary

This chapter has

- explored differing theoretical approaches to the family
- examined in detail research work on the family
- proposed the concept of the democratic family as the most positive environment for children

legal mandate at local, regional and national levels. As the chapter unfolds we will see that the State is complex and diverse in the way that it operates:

> in making sense of the Advanced Capitalist State, it is essential from the outset to recognize the incredible diversity of state forms amongst those nations that make up the advanced capitalist world. (McGrew, 1992, 67)

Mann describes how:

> The State can assess and tax our income and wealth at source, without our consent or that of our neighbours or kin; it can enforce its will within the day almost anywhere in its domain... The State penetrates everyday life more than did any historical state. (in McGrew, 1992, 67)

In this chapter we will aim to demonstrate how diverse the State is by giving examples from modern, liberal, Western societies; and the debates will also be illustrated with examples from different State forms, including totalitarian governments. We will see that both forms of government – liberal and totalitarian – are proactive in their attempts to shape and influence childhood.

The State and childhood

It is argued here that in recent years the modern Western State has taken an increasingly active position in relation to childhood. This may be for a number of reasons:

(a) The State may focus on childhood increasingly because it has less influence on other policy areas. In the United Kingdom in the 1960s, for example, the State ran many industries and services directly – including steel, the docks and the railways. This is no longer the case; thus, the State may seek to influence society in different ways.

(b) The nation State has also lost influence because of the impact of globalization. Many decisions taken by global private enterprises or by global bodies, such as the International Monetary Fund, reduce the impact of national government policy within their own nations. Again the State may feel that it can maintain its influence through policies that focus on childhood.

(c) Globalization has an impact on childhood in another way as well. As global economic competition increases nation states have to be nimble and innovative in making sure that their nation state does not lose out in the global stakes. Governments see investment in childhood – in the education, health and socialization of children – as one key way of making sure that they are best able to meet the forthcoming challenges of globalization.

For these, and perhaps for other reasons, the modern Western State has recently been increasing State intervention in childhood.

In addition to the trends identified above contemporary society has also become increasingly individualized, which has contributed to an increasing focus on childhood. This trend has had a profound impact for the State and families as reflected upon by Beck Gernshiem as follows:

> When we speak of 'individualization', we always have a two-fold tendency in mind. On the one hand, the traditional social relationships, bonds and belief systems that used to determine people's lives in the narrowest detail have been losing more and more of their meaning. From family unit and village community through region and religion to class, corporation and gender role, what used to provide a framework and rules for people's daily lives have become increasingly brittle. New space and new options have thereby opened up for individuals. Now men and women can and should, may and must, decide for themselves how to shape their lives – within certain limits, at least.
>
> On the other hand, individualization means that people are linked into the institutions of the labour market and welfare state, educational system, legal system, state bureaucracy, and so on, which have emerged together with modern society. These institutions produce various regulations – demands, instructions, entitlements – that are typically addressed to individuals rather than the family as a whole. And the crucial feature of these new regulations is that they enjoin the individual to lead a life of his or her own beyond any ties to the family or other groups – or sometimes even to shake off such ties and to act without referring to them. (Beck Gernsheim, 2002, ix)

We can see in this analysis why there might be more focus on the individual 'child' as a carrier of the future and to be positioned to make the life choices that Beck Gernsheim refers to. This contrasts to earlier approaches where the child might have been seen more as part of a group – be that group a particular social class, a geographical entity or a religious movement, for example. Today the focus is increasingly on the individual as the architect of their own destiny.

As a concrete example of how the State has shown an active interest in childhood we explore examples from the English policy from 2003 to 2010 – which illustrates proactive policies towards childhood. The new policies emerged from 2003 onwards under the banner of 'Every Child Matters' (DfES, 2003): the phrase itself reflects Beck Gernsheim's argument well. This

Every Child Matters (see www.everychildmatters.gov.uk) policy stream will be first explained and then critically analysed.

Every Child Matters

In 2003 the Labour government embarked on the most ambitious programme to reform and restructure the experience of English childhood – this programme consists of a wide range of policy initiatives and a major piece of legislation, the Children Act 2004. It will be argued here that a number of key themes emerge from this programme:

- It represents the most ambitious programme of State intervention in England ever, and probably one of the most heavily interventionist programmes in the contemporary international scene.
- The programme invested vast amounts of money in reinventing childhood – or perhaps, more precisely, invested in the salaries of professionals working with children.
- The programme has significant progressive elements – including practical and emotional support for children and families, a significant investment in early childhood care and many initiatives relating to children 'looked after' by the State (see Chapter 8).
- The programme also, simultaneously, contains strong elements of social regulation – in particular through the utilization of concept of outcomes, the surveillance of children and information generation and storage.

The perceived need for the Every Child Matters emerged from a number of factors. Most often it is linked to the death of a young black African girl called Victoria Climbié, although there is evidence that the policy direction existed prior to this (see Frost and Parton, 2009). Victoria died at the hands of her aunt and the aunt's boyfriend. Victoria had been sent to England, via France, from the Ivory Coast in Africa. Her parents felt that her life and educational chances would be enhanced in England. Victoria died at the age of 8 having suffered a long regime of starvation, deprivation and violence from her so-called carers (see Laming, 2003).

The State response to this followed a pattern that had been established earlier – a public inquiry followed by a call for legal and organizational change. The British State had taken a similar approach to the death of Dennis O'Neill in 1946, and to the death of Maria Colwell in 1973 (see Parton, 1985). Below we explore Nigel Parton's research which explored how legislation, policy and practice react to individual child deaths.

Examples of research – deconstructing moral panics about child abuse

Nigel Parton undertook one of the most influential pieces of research ever published on 'the politics of child abuse'. Parton examines the events around the death of Maria Colwell in England in 1973, and the publication of the subsequent inquiry the following year.

His core argument is that

> The way the problem [of child abuse] has been socially constructed has been based on a very particular set of assumptions and explanations. The medical model with its emphasis on individual 'disease', 'treatment', 'identification' and 'prevention' has been dominant. This has been crucial in influencing what we do about the problem and the way in which we do it. Nor has this been a chance development, for changes in the economy, the state and wider society have been central, together with the intervention of certain professional, organisational and political interests. (1985, x)

Parton then is keen to locate the particular events about the death of Maria in the wider social context:

> I argue that debates about the nature of child abuse and what to do about it are in essence not technical but political debates about the good society, and the relationship between the family and the state. (1985, xi)

His argument is clearly political as he relates the issue of child abuse to

> class, inequality and poverty both in terms of prevalence and severity. (1985, 175)

By using the idea of 'moral panic' (first deployed by Cohen, 'a condition, episode, person or group of persons emerges to become defined as a threat to societal values and interests' (1973, 9), Parton is able to locate the concerns about Maria in a wider context:

> It thus is important to see how far the panic about child abuse was related to a more general moral panic at the time, and how far it symbolised a 'more widespread social morass' in British society in the early 1970s. (1985, 72)

Reflections on the research

It will be clear to the reader how the concerns of Parton clearly overlap with the concerns of this book.

In the United Kingdom there have been many examples of individual child deaths leading to large-scale organizational and legal change – Dennis O'Neill, Maria Colwell and the more recent death of 'Baby Peter' all provide examples of tragic deaths leading to major policy change.

Activity 1

Why do individual child deaths sometimes lead to major legislative, policy and practice shifts?

⇨

> ## Activity 2
> What are the possible criticisms that can be made of basing such changes on individual child deaths?

Parton has explored policy responses to individual child deaths, utilizing the concept of 'moral panic' as a major explanatory framework. As we have seen this was destined to happen again following the death of Victoria Climbié. The Every Child Matters policy partially flowed from her death and was based around two key principles:

(a) That there are five outcomes that can be improved for children and young people. These are as follows:
  - Be Healthy
  - Stay Safe
  - Enjoy and Achieve
  - Make a Positive Contribution
  - Achieve Economic Well-being

(b) That the method for delivering these is enhanced coordination of State services for children and young people through integrated working.

Here we see two ideas coming together. First the idea of the 'whole' child identified through the five outcomes – this is the holistic child as opposed to the 'educated child', the 'healthy child' or the 'abused child', for example. These five outcomes, it follows, can only be delivered by a joined-up State response – symbolized by the formation of the Department for Children, Schools and Families in 2007 and the push towards multi-professional, or integrated working to achieve these outcomes (Frost, 2005). The DCSF was renamed in May, 2010, by the Coalition government as simply the Department for Education, arguably Symbolizing a shift away from the integrated working approach.

> ## Example of research – integrated professional working with children
>
> This study examines the effects of organizational characteristics, including organizational climate and inter organizational coordination, on the quality and outcomes of children's services systems.
>
> ⇨

The researchers utilized a quasi-experimental, longitudinal design to assess the effects of increasing inter-organizational services coordination in public children's services agencies in the United States of America. The research team collected both qualitative and quantitative data, over a 3-year period, analysing the services provided to 250 children by 32 public children's service offices in 24 countries in Tennessee.

The researchers have a central focus on what they identify as 'organizational climate'. This concept is an attempt to capture the motivation and support for individual workers. The researchers used low levels of conflict, high levels of cooperation, the existence of role clarity and staff being able to exercise personal discretion as measures of a positive 'organizational climate'.

They also measure outcomes for children and inter-organizational coordination. Inter-organizational coordination was measured using the concepts of authorization, responsibility and monitoring. These concepts were defined as follows:

> Authorization was measured as the number of separate authorizations required for a child to receive services from multiple services. The fewer required, the greater the co-ordination. Responsibility was measured as the number of individuals responsible for ensuring that needed services were delivered to a child. The lower the number, the greater the co-ordination. Monitoring was measured as the proportion of those monitoring services for each child who also provided service to the child. Because co-ordination requires a separation of these responsibilities, lower proportions represent greater co-ordination. (1998, 410)

Their data suggests that 'organizational climate' is

> the primary predictor of positive service outcomes (the children's improved psychosocial functioning) and a significant predictor of service quality. In contrast, inter-organizational co-ordination had a negative effect on service quality and no effect on outcomes. (1998, 401)

The researchers therefore conclude that

> Efforts to improve children's services systems should focus on positive organizational climates rather than on increasing inter-organizational services co-ordination. This is important because many large-scale efforts to improve children's services systems have focused on inter-organizational co-ordination with little success and none to date have focused on organizational climate. (1998, 401)

Reflections on the research

Glisson and Hemmelgarn are clearly very sceptical about the positive impact of greater coordination. They focus instead on 'organizational climate' as the key definer of how effective professionals are in working with children.

⇨

Activity 1
Why might the State think that improving outcomes for children be dependent on improved integration of services?

Activity 2
What do you think the views of children might be on integrated professional working?

We can see here that despite how keen modern States are on developing integrated working, the example of research above suggests that there is room for scepticism about this development.

Modern states are reflexive in the sense that they spend a lot of time and money thinking about, researching, planning and implementing their actions. Recent theory has argued that States are not simply structures that respond in a predetermined manner – but rather they can plan and think strategically, adjusting their actions in response to challenges and circumstances. In terms of children this approach was embodied in the Children's Plan of 2007 (DCSF), the first such plan ever published in England. It emphasized how integrated working, led through 'workforce reform' could deliver the five outcomes. As we have seen the Department for Children, Schools and Families (DCSF) had been formed in June, 2007, to lead this integrated effort.

Every Child Matters – a critique

Having explored Every Child Matters, as an illustrative programme, it is now important that we critically reflect on the programme and the impact it has on children and young people. Here we take the opportunity to reflect on some of the strengths and weaknesses of the Every Child Matters programme.

(a) Strengths

As we have already argued the Every Child Matters programme is enormously significant. The politicians, civil servants and policy makers behind the policy reflect an optimistic view of the State. They believe that the liberal democratic state can deliver real improvements in the lives of children and young people. Here we distance our argument from some critics who view Every Child Matters as an instrument of control and surveillance – a weapon used against children and their families (see Garret, 2009, for example). Every Child Matters has delivered enormous resources for children and young people. Sometimes these are real and tangible – in the form of say children's centres and the Child Trust Fund (which holds money in bank accounts for newly born children and includes extra payments for poorer children). Sometimes these improvements have been in the form of increased participation of young people in policy making and working with professionals. These developments tend to be underplayed by those who over emphasize the negative aspects of Every Child Matters. At central and local government level the real and authentic voices of young people are heard, and sometimes listened to, by those formulating policy and practice. The actual impact of this on outcomes of all these initiatives cannot be usefully commented on at the moment – the results will take sometime to be seen. It would be counter-intuitive to say the least of the efforts of thousands of professionals up and down the country made no impact on the outcomes for children.

(b) Issues and challenges

Like all policies, however progressive, Every Child Matters is vulnerable to a number of critiques. Here we will focus on three issues – the issue of surveillance and information sharing, the impact of the five outcomes and the impact of factors outside the immediate policy field of Every Child Matters.

Surveillance

A feature of late-modern societies is increasing surveillance of citizens. This has technological aspects as new technology provides the infrastructure that enables enhanced surveillance to be possible. It also has political aspects, that is that the political will exists to subject citizens to new and increasing forms of surveillance. The most evident example of this in day-to-day life takes the form of CCTV (closed-circuit television) in our streets.

Specifically in terms of ECM there are at least four forms of surveillance:

- Contact Point

Contact Point is an electronic record of *every* child in England – some 11 million records. This holds basic information on every child and additional information where the child is being worked with by specific State agencies. Specified State employees have access to the information with the intention of them being able to ascertain if other professionals are working with the same child. This was perceived as an issue in the death of Victoria Climbié. Contact Point was abolished by the English Coalition government on 6 August 2010, thus illustrating their different sets of ideology around state intervention in childhood by 'rolling back the State'.

- Information sharing

A related perceived issue contributing to the death of Victoria Climbié was the lack of effective information sharing between professionals. The programme has been utilized to encourage professionals to share information across professional boundaries. This can create a web of information around the child and their family, where, for example, a housing tenancy might be lost due to involvement in antisocial behaviour.

- Early intervention

One of the key themes of Every Child Matters is early intervention – the operating theory here is that in order to prevent problems getting worse as the child gets older it is preferable to intervene as early as possible. This crucially involves gathering information so that the child is known to the authorities and that appropriate action can be taken. Interventions here can take place before actual problems have emerged, thus raising issues about whether intervention is justifiable.

- Safeguarding

Protecting children from abuse and neglect has been a key theme in improving professional coordination in England, at least since the death of Maria Colwell. Traditionally policy was reactive – at this stage professionals referred to 'child abuse' and responded to specific identified incidences of abuse. This then moved to become 'child protection', suggesting that professionals could be more proactive in protecting children from abuse. In England, in recent years, 'safeguarding' has become the key word. This idea is much more diffuse than 'child abuse' or 'child protection' – it takes a wide-lens view of protecting children, much more extensively by being preventive and pro-active. It provides a safeguarding 'gaze' across the whole of childhood, leading to increased checks on professionals and surveillance of childhood through practice, policy and inspection.

All these initiatives add up to an unprecedented surveillance of childhood. Childhood has become subject to integrated teams of professionals, sharing information and intervening early to ensure that children are 'safeguarded'.

The social historian Hendrick has argued that the following stages can be perceived when we examine how children have been understood since the 1680s:

- The Natural child
- The Romantic child
- The Evangelical child
- The Factory child
- The Delinquent child

- The Schooled child
- The Psycho-medical child
    (for detailed outlines of each view of childhood see Hendrick, 1994, 21–37)

Given the reflections on Every Child Matters it can perhaps be argued that in the twenty-first century the modern Western Child can be seen as 'the normalized child', or 'the child under surveillance'?

Outcomes and normalization

As we have seen the historian Ariès argued that once childhood was 'discovered' it was utilized as a means of normalizing childhood. By normalizing we mean that a dominant 'way of being' emerges and governments want their citizens to aspire to these norms. In a sense then, effective parenting does the government's work for it – if as a parent you aspire to the established norms then the government can leave you to get on with the task of parenting. This process also creates 'the other': those groups who do not aspire to the norm. These groups may actively reject a norm, for example groups who disagree with compulsory State schooling, or they may be unable to achieve them, perhaps due to disadvantage or personal challenges, such as drug abuse.

The English example of the 'five outcomes' can thus be seen as an example of 'normalization', of creating what Ariès called 'the well-bred child'. The State is now involved in generating the five outcomes for all the children of the nation – interventions such as 'staying safe' which tended to apply to small, specified groups of children are now utilized to guide policy for all children.

Thus far we have examined surveillance and normalization as potential critiques of ambitious State programmes such as Every Child Matters. A final matter for consideration is whether such programmes are naive in assuming that the State can have a major impact on childhood in a free market society, where global market forces are very powerful and arguably can undermine the best intentions of the State.

Such factors might include commercial forces, such as the advertising of 'junk food', which undermine State attempts to promote healthy eating. Another force may be the media and information technology, which, for example, promotes images of sexuality which can be accessed by children.

In terms of the outcome 'being economically active' it can be undermined by global economic forces, as we saw in 2008–2010 with the recession triggered by the so-called 'credit crunch'. While governments attempted to mitigate the impact of the recession, the large-scale global forces were beyond the control of any national or international State forces. Thus while a given local government authority might launch an anti-child poverty initiative in its own area, this can be quickly undermined by, say, a factory closure which leads to widespread unemployment and economic distress in an area.

In this section we have explored the Every Child Matters initiative as an example of how the modern State pro-actively engages with childhood. We have argued that such initiatives have many strengths which have the potential to increase the quality of life of children and can promote active participation by children in the policy process. However, we have also outlined how tendencies such as surveillance, normalization and wider social factors can undermine the impact of ambitious State programmes. We have also reflected that the ambitions of the State may be limited and deflected by the power of the market and commercial forces.

The State and its impact on childhood

We now move on to look specifically at how the State can have an impact on childhood. We have argued that the State today reflexively attempts to govern and shape childhood, and we have explored one example, in the form of England's Every Child Matters.

In the following section we examine two important research projects which explore how different State initiatives impact on childhood. First, we explore the important and influential work of Linda Gordon on how philanthropic, or charitable, organizations have an impact on children and their relationships with parents. Second, we look at the work of Urie Bronfenbrenner, who addresses specifically one of the main concerns of this book – how can the State and political interventions shape childhood and how this can vary in different political contexts.

Research example – re-envisioning interventions around child abuse

Linda Gordon produced one of the most valuable and readable pieces of research demonstrating how official interventions work with families and children. Her research involved a detailed study of the records kept by social work agencies in the Boston area between 1880 and 1960. By submitting the case files to meticulous analysis and by

⇨

reading them as a feminist historian she gives us a fascinating insight into the detail of how official organizations, children and families actually relate to each other in actual, concrete situations.

Gordon states that

> the central argument of [her] book is that family violence has been historically and politically constructed. (1986, 3)

For example, she reconstructs family violence cases from the last quarter of the nine-teenth century. She shows how cruelty to children tended to focus on the male in the household – very often a recent immigrant. The social workers tended to be judge-mental of his drinking – the negligent, feckless male was seen as a concrete social problem.

Gordon argues that the social work interventions she explored

> sought to reconstruct the family along lines that altered the old patri-archy...and replace it with a modern version of male supremacy. This new system included state regulation limiting parental rights and prescribing new standards for child-raising. Children were to be disciplined with patience and indulgence. (1989, x)

Gordon argues that this modernization of the family had real benefits for women and children – therefore it is mistaken to see social work-type interventions as simply forms of social control.

Reflections on the research

Activity 1
Gordon argues that social work was influential in giving a wider message about how a modern family should function. Could it be said that contemporary social work func-tions in the same way?

Activity 2
Gordon argues that it is a mistake to see social work simply as social control. How can social workers concretely improve the lives of children?

Gordon's work is important in helping us reflect on what social workers actu-ally do and how they can help give women and children more control over their lives. While Gordon explores the work of a charitable or philanthropic organization, Donzelot analyses the role of such bodies as follows:

> Philanthropy...is not to be understood as a naively apolitical term signifying a private intervention in the sphere of so-called social problems, but must be con-sidered as a deliberately de-politicizing strategy for establishing public services

and facilities at a sensitive point midway between private initiative and the state. (1979, 55)

Here Donzelot provides an explanation of the connections between the philanthropic bodies explored by Gordon and the State.

The research of Urie Bronfenbrenner paints on a larger canvas than Linda Gordon – comparing childhood in the two most powerful countries in the world at the time of his work. His work is important as it stands fairly much alone in comparing two vastly different social systems and the impact this can have on children. At the time of his research the United States of America was the powerful market economy in the world, and the Soviet Union (or the Union of Soviet Socialist Republics) was the most powerful centralized, socialist society. What difference did this make to children? Bronfenbrenner explores childhood in these two contrasting political systems – the liberal market society of the United States of America, contrasted with the centralized, totalitarian government of the former Soviet Union.

Example of research: two contrasting constructions of childhood

Research by Urie Bronfenbrenner provides us with a classic example of how the construction of childhood can vary depending on the attitude of the State towards childhood. Bronfenbrenner conducted three studies which contributed to his study of childhood in the United States of America and the Union of Soviet Socialist Republics (USSR). Bronfenbrenner argues that one way of judging a society is to use the criterion of 'the concern of one generation for the next' (1974, 1). He argues that the main concern of his book is to ask how the child 'becomes of social being' (1974, 2).

Bronfenbrenner states that the two societies vary in where the primary responsibility lays for raising the child:

> in the US, we ordinarily think of this responsibility as centred in the family, with the parents as the central agents of child rearing...not so in the USSR where the emphasis is on a collective centred system of child rearing. (1974, 3–4)

Having described the role of the school, the youth organization and the family Bronfenbrenner concludes

> This then is the process of collective upbringing. For a Westerner, it may seem a far cry from the world of the family with its informal, personalised, and yet private expressions of parental affection and authority. Yet, for the Soviet Child, there is considerable psychological continuity between the two con-

$\Rightarrow$

texts. Both are strong sources of security, support, and satisfaction: in both deviance is interpreted as emotional betrayal and is responded to be withdrawal and acceptance of mobilisation of guilt. (1974, 69)

The Soviet child then is collectivized and raised in State dominated settings. This contrasts significantly with the child raised in the US setting.

Bronfenbrenner argues that in the United States of America the idea of the child being raised predominantly by the family is also in the past:

Urbanisation has reduced the extended family to a nuclear one with only two adults. (1974, 97)

One result of this is that the child is propelled into a peer group:

the vacuum left by the withdrawal of parents and adults from the lives of children is filled with an undesired – and possibly undesirable – substitute of an age segregated peer group. (1974, 102)

Bronfenbrenner concludes that

If the Russians have gone too far in subjecting the child and his peer group to conformity to a single set of values imposed by the adult society, perhaps we [the Americans] have reached the point of diminishing returns in allowing excessive autonomy and in failing to utilize the constructive potential of the peer group in developing social responsibility and consideration for others … what is called for is greater involvement of parents, and other adults, in the lives of children, and – conversely – greater involvement of children in responsibility for their own family, community and society at large. (1974, 166–167)

Activity 1

Think of two contrasting countries today. How does childhood differ in these two countries and why?

Activity 2

Bronfenbrenner demonstrates how different political systems have an impact on children. How does this actually happen? How does the State and the social system actually have an impact on childhood?

Bronfenbrenner demonstrates how the 'big picture' – the social and political system – has a real and researchable impact on the everyday life of individual children. Other theorists have agreed with Bronfenbrenner, including the communitarian Etzioni, who argues that

Nobody likes to admit it, but between 1960 and 1990 American society allowed children to be devalued, while the golden call of 'making it' was put on a high pedestal. (1993, 63)

We have seen that the State side of the 'triangle' explored in this book is clearly influential in the impact it can have on children and families.

In a sense Bronfenbrenner explored two extreme ends of the spectrum. Coontz argues for the importance of such studies as follows:

> Understanding the specificity of social location and the importance of context…directs our attention to the tension between the institutional or historical constraints under which people operate and the tool kit of personal cultural and social resources they use to make choices. (2000, 294)

Modern social democracies probably fall somewhere between these two extremes explored by Bronfenbrenner, as they are market-based societies that attempt to provide elements of welfare and social security for their citizens.

Parton analyses the challenges for such contemporary liberal States as follows:

> The emergence of the social and its central concern with the family was a positive solution to a major social problem posed for the liberal state. Namely – how can the state establish the rights of individual children while promoting the family as the natural sphere for raising children and hence not intervening in all families and thus reducing its autonomy? (1991, 12)

This concisely expresses the key problems that will be explored in this book.

Activities

The following activities are designed to help reflect back on some of the key concerns over the chapter as a whole.

Activity 1

We have argued that childhood can be very different in different nation states. This has been demonstrated by the work of Urie Bronfenbrenner, for example. Can you compare childhood in two countries you are aware of? How does childhood differ? If there are differences how can you explain these differences?

Activity 2

We have explored the English government's Every Child Matters programme. It is not clear at the time of writing if the programme has brought about major changes. Can the State change childhood? Are there issues that are so private and so personal (e.g. sexual behaviour) that are beyond the reach of the State?

Summary

This chapter has

- explored the nature of the relationship between the State and childhood
- analysed how official interventions attempt to shape and influence childhood
- provided a case study of how two particular contrasting States (the United States of America and the former Soviet Union) produced two different kinds of childhood

Further reading

Fox Harding, L. (1991) *Perspectives in Child Care Policy.* London: Longman

Fox Harding provides a theoretical framework for exploring the relationship between the family and the State. Her framework includes laissez faire, protectionist, family support and children's rights 'value perspectives' in relation to child and family policy.

Laming, H. (2003) *The Victoria Climbié Report: Report of an Inquiry by Lord Laming.* London: The Stationery Office

This is an influential report that provides a harrowing account of the events surrounding the death of Victoria. The report was influential in shaping English child welfare policy for the next decade.

Parton, N. (1991) *Governing the Family: Child Care, Child Protection and the State.* Basingstoke: Macmillan

This is an important study that utilizes social theory to explore the challenges of governing the family in modern liberal states. It allows the reader to trace Parton's work building on his 1985 book that is utilized earlier as an 'example of research'.

Research details

Deconstructing moral panics about child abuse

Nigel Parton has analysed one of the key incidences of child death in the United Kingdom – the death of Maria Colwell. Using the idea of moral panic Parton provides a sociological analysis of the reaction to, and the changes resulting from, the report into Maria's death.

Parton, N. (1985) *The Politics of Child Abuse.* Basingstoke: Macmillan

Integrated professional working with children

This is one of the most important studies ever undertaken of the impact of integrated professional working with children and young people. It argues that the evidence of integrated working, or 'inter-organizational coordination', on the welfare of children is weak. They identify 'inter-organizational climate' as more important in promoting the best interests of children.

Glisson, C. and Hemmelgarn, A. (2003) 'The Effects of Organisational Climate and Inter organizational coordination on the Quality and Outcomes of Children's Service systems', *Child Abuse and Neglect,* 22 (5), 401–421

Re-envisioning interventions around child abuse

Linda Gordon analysed social work case files dating back to the 1880s in the United States of America. Her detailed feminist reading of the material indicates how the interventions attempted to modernize how families worked, and sometimes worked to the benefit of women and children.

Gordon, L. (1986) *Heroes of Their Own Lives: The Politics and History of Family Violence.* London: Virago

Two contrasting constructions of childhood

Bronfenbrenner, the originator of ecological theory, provides a fascinating study of childhood in the United States of America and the former Soviet Union at a time they were the two pre-eminent world powers. His study contrasts childhood in a collectivized, socialist State with a more individualized market society.

Bronfenbrenner, U. (1974) *Two Worlds of Childhood.* Harmondsworth: Penguin

Part 3
Implications for Children's Lives

Being a Child in the Modern World

Chapter Outline

Introduction and key questions

As we have outlined earlier, children have been the object of a considerable amount of research since the emergence of childhood as a defined social group. The term 'object' is selected deliberately here – as much social and psychological research has treated children as passive objects, people to be observed, measured and classified (see the classic research of Piaget (1959), for example).

Smith defines such developmental approaches as those

> which emphasise the programmed and sequential qualities of cognitive, emotional and behavioural development throughout childhood...Here general differences between individuals of different ages (or 'stages') are emphasised, as well as features which are consistent among children. (2010, 64)

The tradition of treating children as objects began to be challenged in the 1970s when radical views of childhood emerged – such as Ivan Illich's work on 'de-schooling' society (1973) and John Holt's work on children's rights (1975) – which began to see children and young people as more active in shaping their own lives. These trends became more dominant and arguably began to shape social research when the 'new sociology of childhood' emerged in the 1980s (see James et al. 1998, and Jenks, 1996). Thus far in this book we have seen childhood emerge as a high-profile concern of social history, that childhood became more central to the role of the family and that children have been increasingly the focus of State activities and policies. In this chapter we explore what it is like being a child in the modern world.

The following questions will be addressed in this chapter with a focus on childhood:

> How have children been treated as objects?
> How do children resist being treated as objects?
> What does it mean for children to act as active subjects?
> How are children's lives affected by State policies?
> How are some groups of children marginalized by society?

Children as objects

In terms of British legal and social policy we can identify a significant event in children moving from being seen as passive objects to be regarded as self-determining human beings. In the mid-1980s an English area then known as Cleveland was shaken by a series of events around the alleged sexual abuse of children. Over 100 children were taken into care during a short period when they were examined for symptoms of sexual abuse at Middlesbrough General Hospital.

Once the immediate events had unfolded the government asked an established High Court judge, Elizabeth Butler-Sloss, to inquire into these events and she eventually reported in 1986. In many ways the Inquiry signalled a new view of childhood in the United Kingdom. While the details of the events need not concern us here (see Campbell, 1988) what is significant is that Butler-Sloss argued that 'the child is a person, not an object of concern' (1988, 245). She felt that the medical and social service organizations had seen children as objects where the role of the State was to ascertain whether or not the child had been abused. This perception of children as more than simply objects provides a link through political, social, legal and research approaches to childhood through the last quarter of the twentieth century. Before moving on to emerging paradigms of childhood we will first explore how children have traditionally been seen as passive objects.

Social science an   icial statistics have, at least since Victorian times,
been keen to measure   assess childhood. Children have been measured not
only in the obvious ser.   – of their height and weight – but also in terms of
their 'development', thei. intelligence' and more recently their 'performance'
in school exams. During t. e late nineteenth century it led to the emergence of
what Donzelot identifies as the 'psy' professions – psychologists, social workers and others paid to assess and measure children. While measurements and
assessments present themselves as being 'scientific and 'true' they are actually
profoundly social phenomena. Measuring children serves a social function –
it treats them as passive objects, future human beings who can be assessed by
independent and superior adults using scientific methods. These measures
are never innocent – by which we mean that they always serve a purpose and
have a goal. The purpose is often to assess, to classify and to segment and then
to utilize these categories as a basis for intervention in the lives of children.

The style of measurement, of course, changes over time – for example from
the bearded Victorian philanthropist determined to improve the lives of children to the contemporary Scholastic Aptitude Tests (SATs) that are utilized
in England to assess children and to rank their schools in league tables as a
result. What the measurements have in common is that the child is seen as
a passive object that is required to comply and cooperate while being measured. The child is seen as a category, as 'data', to be represented in a report or
a league table.

Contemporary children are measured more than children have ever been
through school tests, throughout their lives in terms of achievement and
development, and are increasingly subject to surveillance on the streets and
shopping centres through CCTV and legal restrictions. In England between
1997 and 2010 under the New Labour government we saw the introduction
of such policies as the creation of 'dispersal areas' which enabled the police
to direct individuals to leave an area and be barred from it for up to 24 hours
and Anti-Social Behaviour Orders, which could place a wide range of restrictions on individual behaviour.

Again in all these categories children are seen as passive – as objects ready
to be measured, classified and controlled through the adult gaze.

Children as objects – an example of State policy

We have already seen that children are perceived as carriers of the future
and that State agencies often think that large-scale political and ideological
projects can be achieved through interventions in childhood – the Hitler

Youth would be an obvious and dramatic example of this way of thinking. The research example below provides another dramatic narrative of how children can be seen as passive carriers of political intentions. The example comes from China under Mao, and the researchers illustrate how the events have a major impact on young people's lives.

Research example: 'send down' – a powerful State intervention

This important piece of research offers us an example of analysis of a situation where there is a totalitarian state which has a very powerful impact on the lives of children and young people.

In China in 1968 the leader of the country, Mao Zedong, stated that it was necessary for 'the educated youth to go to the countryside, and to be re-educated by the poor peasants' (Zhou and Hou, 1999, 12). This resulted in what was effectively the enforced migration of millions of children from the city to the country. The average stay was for 6 years, while their parents remained in the city. The researchers interviewed these children in 1993 and 1994 and assessed the impact of what was known as the 'send down' to the country on their life course and life chances.

The researchers found, perhaps unsurprisingly, that these events had a major impact on the life course of the children who experienced the 'send down'.

The researchers demonstrate that

> the 12 year send down mobilization in China has fundamentally changed the life course of a generation of urban youth...Our study points to the decisive role of the state and state policy shifts that disrupt and restructure individuals' life course. (1999, 31)

The researchers found that the experience had an adverse impact on all social groups, but they also demonstrate that those of higher social status were able to get their children back sooner and were able to gain educational advantage when compared with other social groups. They also found that marriage and childbirth were delayed in the send down group as they took time to regain control over their own lives. This illustrates the profound impact of State policy on the most personal decisions of individual lives.

The researchers conclude that

> the legacy of the send down episode is likely to continue to influence the life course of the children of the Cultural Revolution and, more importantly, the future course of changes in China. (1999, 33)

Reflections on the research

This is important research that powerfully demonstrates the impact of a totalitarian State on the individual lives of children, and the long-term impact of such State policies.

⇨

Activity 1

Can you think of any other examples where State policies have had such a dramatic impact on the lives of children?

Activity 2

How were children treated in this example? Is there any evidence that they were consulted or given a voice? How can research help in giving people a voice?

This Chinese example allows us to reflect on the dramatic impact of State policies on children and their experience of childhood. We can see how children can be constructed as passive objects to be acted upon, and who thus become 'carriers' of major political and ideological objectives.

It is worth noting that Western-style contemporary governments can intervene in ways that seem equally authoritarian. In 2007 the Australian State took an extraordinary decision. Following a report entitled 'Little Children are Sacred' they mounted what is called as 'the intervention' in the North Territory. They argued that the Aboriginal population in Northern Territory were involved in the widespread abuse of their children, alongside child sexual exploitation, domestic violence and the use of pornography. They blamed this largely on the abuse of alcohol by adult males (see Young, 2008, for competing forms of explanation of these events). As a result the Australian State decided to withdraw all State benefits and replace them with vouchers – that could only be spent for food, clothing and other essentials. Using our triangle of relationships we can see here that the State is intervening in the line that connects the child and parents. The State is using its power extensively to regulate the role of the parent, in the name of safeguarding children and their childhood.

Children and resistance

It is important to note that children often resist State and parental initiatives, and we should be careful never to cast them as passive. Children are never passive – they can avoid, resist and protest. We can all remember from our own childhoods how we kept secrets, disobeyed and sometimes actively revolted, in order to maintain some privacy and control over our own lives.

The French social philosopher Michel Foucault has observed that wherever there is power there is also resistance. This is a powerful observation in relation to efforts to measure and classify children.

We can provide examples of children resisting in three main ways – passive individual resistance, active individual resistance and strategic collective resistance which can be seen in Figure 5.1.

	Individual	Collective
Passive	Refusal to take part in school activity or assessment	Large-scale refusal to participate
Active	Refusal to comply with school uniform policy and adopt alternative	School strikes and protests
Strategic	Determination to pursue a career adults disapprove of for example rock musician	Formation of protest groups for example collective groups of children in care

Figure 5.1 Forms of resistance by children

Passive resistance is experienced everyday in schools and other settings – where children are seen as uncooperative, stroppy or non-compliant. Children might refuse to answers questions, complete homework, or take part in activities – all these are forms of resistance to authority. Even relatively minor forms of 'role distance' – such as ensuring that the school tie hangs loose around the neck – are significant, where children can be seen as resisting the imposition of adult regimes of power.

More active resistance might involve ways of avoiding adult regimes. The author, for example, once witnessed a group of young women in a children's home who had devised a secret language through which they could talk to each other without staff understanding.

Strategic resistance would involve more collective campaigns – movements of children designed to change social conditions. The organized campaign of young people in the care system provides an example of this form of collectivized social resistance. Famously the children of a Norfolk school, Burston, went on strike in support of their sacked teacher – a strike that lasted from 1914 until 1939! (Edwards, 1974)

Children as active subjects

With powerful social movements around the United Nations Convention on the Rights of the Child, the key role of non-governmental organizations such as Save the Children, children organizing themselves and the work of progressive adults, we have seen what Jones (2009) identifies as 'emerging' approaches to childhood. The example of research in the box below demonstrates how the interface between the State, families and childhood is being transformed by these 'emerging' approaches that begin to construct children as more active agents of their own lives.

Example of research: giving children a voice in family decision-making

This study examined how children acted as active participants in family group conferences, a system designed to give children and families more influence over decision-making where there is proposed State intervention around family problems. The following methods were adopted:

> The research was a qualitative study of 17 family meetings. Twenty-five children and young people were interviewed within 1 month of the meeting and 13 were re-interviewed 6 months later. Adult participants were also interviewed. (Holland and O'Neill, 2006, 91)

The researchers utilized a wide range of research methods which were designed to maximize participation by children including use of play-based methods:

> The aim of such techniques is to provide a more child-centred and participative approach to the traditional verbal interview, which might to help address adult–child power imbalances. (2006, 98)

While the researchers are generally optimistic about the impact on young people's participation there remain risks and challenges. For example, one respondent commented:

> *Darren*: I didn't have chance to say half the things I wanted to. I didn't have chance to throw in as many points as I wanted to, sort of thing. I was trying but I was getting interrupted, shouted at, screamed at all the time

The researchers reflect that

> Here, Darren reports that there was a gap between his expectation of being able to participate in the meetings, promoted by the professional facilitators ('I was told I was going to be the most powerful person there') and his actual experience in the private family time when professionals withdrew. Here we have the first risk regarding children's participation: not all adults will respond to professional entreaties to listen to the child…although it must be emphasized that Darren's experience was not shared by the majority. (2006, 100)

The researchers go on to give a more positive example:

> *Interviewer*: Was anyone else powerful?
> *Brittaney*: Me.

⇨

> *Interviewer:* You felt powerful did you?
> *Brittaney:* Yes, because at first I didn't want to speak and then I said what I wanted to say (2006, 100)

This is a good example of the child feeling more powerful, an experience shared by about two-thirds of the sample.

The researchers summarize their work as follows:

> the potential risks and benefits of enabling children to participate in formal family decision-making, it might be seen that, while a few of the potential risks were realized for some of the young people, the benefits of participating appeared to outweigh these risks for most of them. (2006, 103)

They argue that while 'our findings must be regarded as exploratory' it remains the case that

> In the family group conferences in our study, young people were generally enabled to participate in family decision-making and most felt positive about the experience. The children distinguished between the experiences of being listened to and feeling influential, demonstrating that power does not necessarily follow participation. (2006, 108)

In terms of the primary concerns of this book the researchers summarize their position as follows:

> It should be acknowledged that the family is a site of oppression for some children. These findings remind us that there are risks as well as benefits when children's participation is encouraged. Additionally, there are possibly some unresolved, and perhaps irresolvable, tensions between a process that promotes the concept of family unity alongside a philosophy of children's views having priority. The findings reported here, in our view, contribute to the growing literature that problematizes the notion of children's participation while also supporting the principles behind it. (2006, 109)

Reflections on research

The research, therefore, provides some useful reflections on the relationship between the State, families and childhood and how existing power relations are shifting and being challenged. It also demonstrates that such shifts are complex and difficult in practice.

Activity 1
How would you assess the strengths and weaknesses of the family group conference in transforming power relations between the State, family and childhood?

Activity 2
Can you think of any other concrete initiative such as this that attempt to transform power relations in this way?

The research example on family group conferences is helpful in the sense that it is real and practical in giving a voice to children.

UNICEF is a national body that is committed to giving a voice to children and to making the United Nations Convention on the Rights of the Child (UNCRC) a reality. Their report on the state of childhood in rich countries is significant for this book in a number of ways. It gives us a relatively up-to-date view of children's lives, it allows us to reflect on variations across different nation states and it gives a voice to children, by including subjective measures of their well-being. The box below provides a summary of one significant and groundbreaking UNICEF study.

Example of research: an international study of child well-being

In 2007, UNICEF (the United Nations Children's Fund) published an influential study that compared the state of childhood in 21 'rich countries'. This is an important study as it is methodologically rigorous and allows us to systematically compare the lives of children across different countries. The authors of the report state that

> This *Report Card* provides a comprehensive assessment of the lives and well-being of children and young people in 21 nations in the industrialised world. (2007, 2)

The authors point out that they faced many challenges in gathering their data and argue:

> Acknowledging these limitations, (this report) nonetheless invites debate and breaks new ground by bringing together the best of currently available data and represents a significant step towards a multi-dimensional overview of the state of childhood in a majority of the economically advanced nations of the world. (UNICEF, 2007, 3)

The relevance of the study to this book is that it illustrates one of the points we made in the introduction to this book – that childhood varies geographically. We can see from the UNICEF study that childhood is very different – even in societies that are identified as 'rich' and that seem to be very similar. The UNICEF study is also important because it gives a voice to children, through the measurement of 'subjective well-being'. By utilizing the study we can see that children experience there own lives very differently depending where they live.

The extract from the table below demonstrates the difference between the nominal 'best' country for children to grow up in – the Netherlands – and the lowest country in the table – the United Kingdom.

Dimension	Netherlands (out of 21)	United Kingdom (out of 21)
Average ranking for all 6 dimensions	4.2	18.2
Material well being	10	18
Health and safety	2	12
Educational well-being	6	17
Family + peer relations	3	21
Behaviours and risks	3	21
Subjective well-being	1	20

We can see that the Netherlands is more positive for children on all the dimensions explored. The Report Card states that

> The United Kingdom and the United States find themselves in the bottom third of the rankings for five of the six dimensions reviewed. (2007, 2)

Reflections on the research

The researchers who produced the UNICEF report have demonstrated how the experience of childhood is different in 21 countries.

Activity 1
Why might childhood vary so considerably across different nation states?

Activity 2
Using the evidence in this box how crucial do you think the role of the State is in shaping differences in children's lives?

The UNICEF study is helpful in helping us reflect on the 'social construction' of childhood across different national boundaries. There are, of course, many differences between the countries – some such as climate and location largely beyond the control of people – but the role of the State is arguably crucial here. We can see, for example, that the Scandinavian states, which traditionally have high levels of public expenditure, tend to be towards the top the various league tables. The casual visitor to Mediterranean countries, for example, will soon notice how children are more visible and welcome in the streets and in restaurants, when compared with other Western cultures.

In the following example of research box we explore how children see themselves as more active citizens and how they evaluate being involved in political participation.

Example of research: children and participation in politics

This study is highly relevant to this book as it focuses on the views of children about active participation in the State.

The sample was constructed as follows:

> We selected six primary schools to take part in the study, which were chosen to represent a purposive sample of the diversity of life in Wales. These were selected on the basis of information about the socio-economic, ethnic, geographical and linguistic character of their various locations obtained from a variety of sources. We spoke to a total of 105 children over 3 months, conducting a total of 18 focus groups. The children were drawn from the 8–11 age bracket from a range of social classes, ability ranges, ethnicities, nationalities and linguistic identities. This range was identified by teachers in the schools. Six children from each of year groups 4, 5 and 6 in each school were asked to take part in a focus group where issues such as nationality, locality, civic identity, language, media, race and cultural difference were discussed. There were an equal number of boys and girls, and half the sample of children were able to speak the Welsh language as well as English. (Drakeford et al., 2009, 251)

One key finding of the research is that

> As far as relevant factors are concerned, the children's views were very clear and specific. They tended to focus around the possible impact that a new road would have on their lives, thus, it might be argued, highlighting the direct impact of such measures on children's everyday lives as active citizens. A number of children in our study were able to recount personal experiences of near-accidents in traffic. The road would be important, said Bahira at Highfields, 'because when I was little I was holding my mother's hand and I just ran across this busy road, but luckily, I fell over just by the pavement and this woman stopped like a few centimetres away from me in her car'. Now, living 'on quite a busy road' she 'can't go out'. The effect of traffic on not being allowed out, or not being 'allowed to cross the main road' (Emma at Petersfield) was a recurrent theme in children's responses. (2009, 255–257)

The researchers argue that children express a clear view:

> What seems clear from all this is that children have a clear understanding of 'participatory citizenship'...and locate themselves clearly within that paradigm. Even at the age of 8 or 9, they are able to step outside their own circumstances and consider the importance of others' views...The thread that runs through the very many ways they are able to suggest as vehicles for making their views known is *respect*. (2009, 257)

The children are able to locate themselves in the political process as follows:

> Our research suggests that middle childhood is a period when children are able to identify a wide range of civic agencies and know something about

⇨

how to access the rights that those agencies provide. In operationalizing that access, however, they opt for a range of intermediaries, a process that is context-specific and strengthens as the issue under consideration becomes more serious. (2009, 260)

The researchers summarize their work as follows:

the children showed varying degrees of understanding of different levels of government in Wales. Given that the Welsh Assembly was a very new institution when we collected our data and many Welsh adults seem confused about its role, the children's awareness of the Assembly was encouraging. While declaring a lack of interest in politics in general, the children did in fact engage enthusiastically in discussion of specific issues that they saw affecting their lives. They generally believed they should be consulted on issues that would affect them directly and spoke of using adult intermediaries to feed their views into formal decision-making processes. They generally did not believe that the views of children would (or indeed should) be decisive. Most believed that their views ought to be considered alongside others. What these children seem to expect is that, while their views may not count as decisive, they deserve equal respect with any other views in being taken into account. (2009, 260)

The researchers conclude:

When exploring the connectedness of government to the everyday lives of children, our research suggests that, as far as identity formation is concerned, the impact of civic institutions is calibrated by the extent to which these institutions are able to shape more immediately important parts of a child's experience. (2009, 263)

Activity 1
How can real and effective links be made between children's lives and effective participation in political life?

Activity 2
Can you think of any examples of children playing an active role in political life?

We have seen in the last two examples of research how children can be given a voice – through research focusing on their experiences and through political participation. We now move on to examine groups of children for whom participation is even more complex because of their marginalized position in relation to the rest of society.

Children as marginalized

Some groups of children are marginalized –they exist on the margins of society, 'socially excluded' from the mainstream. Marginalized groups of children are often 'others', viewed as strange and alien.

In the United Kingdom the power of language is demonstrated as marginalized children are often referred to be de-humanizing sets of initials – LAC (looked-after children), NEET (not in education or employment) and UASC (unaccompanied asylum seeking children) being examples of this. We will refer to the last group as unaccompanied children, in order to avoid the UASC abbreviation. This group is arguably the most exposed and exploited group of children in the world today. In terms of our triangle these children exist in isolation from their State of origin and their family, leaving them particularly exposed to the unfettered exercise of power over their lives.

The research example below explores their experience in some detail, alongside that of other children seeking refuge.

Example of research: being a refugee or asylum seeker

Rachel Hek has reviewed the research literature in order to give a voice to unaccompanied children. She explores the tension in British law as to whether these children should be seen as children first or as refugees:

> Many studies have found that refugee children and young people are often not seen as children first, but are dealt with as refugees. These studies point out that refugee children face the same issues as any other children, but that there are also specific and extra issues that need to be taken into account when thinking about appropriate service provision. (2005,1)

Hek demonstrates that where unaccompanied children and young people have been consulted it is clear that they value practical help and assistance:

> They have talked about how important it was to find a placement where they would be welcomed: a reliable legal representative who could deal speedily with their application for asylum and someone who could assist them with their language skills, settling into school or college, and accessing health services. (2005, 116)

It is clear from Hek's work that unaccompanied children share many needs, issues and strengths with other children referred to in this book but they also face a set of particular challenges which mean that they require a specific set of help and intervention. The

⇨

quote below gives voice to a child whose situation echoes that of many other unaccompanied children. It is certainly worth reporting at some length:

> I am very depressed because I miss my own country, I miss my family. I have lost contact with all of them. There are problems in the house: it's cold and dirty and the landlord doesn't care about us, there is also the problem of not knowing how long I am going to be living here, I can't put down roots, I can't try and make a future when I don't know how long I am going to be here and I do want to go back eventually, although I know that my own country is in a state of turmoil. I grew up with war around me and I have never really known normality; in fact this is quite strange coming here and not having to deal with some of the issues I was dealing with in my own country. I have witnessed war since I was a child. I learned to play with pistols and guns. I have seen people dead on the side of the road and now I am reliving it. This makes it really difficult for me to concentrate on learning English. I need to be in a good mood to learn. I need to have a steady life. (Marriott, 2001, in Hek, 2005, 24–25)

Hek summarizes young peoples' views as follows:

> Young people express anxiety about this transition, and say that they have little information and what information they do receive is unclear and confusing. (2005, 49)

Reflection on research

Hek's work illustrates the serious challenges facing unaccompanied children who are vulnerable to significant exploitation.

Activity 1
Do you agree that unaccompanied children form a disadvantaged group? Can you think of other groups of children that seem to be significantly disadvantaged?

Activity 2
How are unaccompanied children 'othered'?

We can see here some of the experiences of unaccompanied and refugee children, as representing one example of marginalized children.

In order to explore this issue further we utilize the work of the Children's Commissioner for England who undertook an unannounced visit to a screening unit established to assess asylum applications from people claiming to be under the age of 18. The initial report outlines the challenging nature of the process:

> Children need to have their basic needs for accommodation, food, cleanliness and rest met before they undergo this intense and lengthy sequence of events. They

also require legal representation and information to help them understand the process better. The oppressive nature of large parts of the asylum process makes it difficult for children to give a full and accurate account of themselves. This may have implications for the decision made on their asylum claim. (11 million, 2008, 12)

These observations are brought to life by a direct quote from a young Ugandan woman, aged 16:

> No one told me what was happening. I had nothing to eat or drink, not even water. I went to the toilet, that's where I got water to drink because at the time you don't have any money...it was really bad. It's how they treat you and deal with the other people and ignore you like you are not there. Then they ask you the same questions over and over again. (11 million, 2008, 4)

Below we report a follow-up visit which gives an insight into the challenging lives facing some specific groups of young people.

Example of research: an Inspection of an Immigration Removal Centre by the Children's Commissioner for England

This review examined the conditions in a centre where children of all ages were detained – the report was a follow up to an earlier visit where grave concerns had been expressed:

> We visited Yarl's Wood Immigration Removal Centre twice. On the first visit we conducted face-to-face interviews with detained adult family members, and held participation sessions with school-aged children. In the following visit we took health and social care professionals to study a sample of medical records and welfare files, in order first to examine in greater detail the issues raised by families, and second, to assess progress following our report in 2009. (2010, 5)

The report is set against the background of the United Nations Convention on the Rights of the Child. The Report notes that

> The removal of the Government's reservation on the UN Convention on the Rights of the Child (UNCRC) is welcome. Article 37(b) of the UNCRC requires that detention is used only as a measure of last resort and for the shortest appropriate period of time...Our evidence [shows] that some children are admitted to Yarl's Wood for prolonged periods, and sometimes repeatedly. (2010, 5)

The visit found that

> the average length of time in detention for children and young people is 14 days, with some children being held for much longer periods. This is unac-

⇨

---

ceptable and further research and debate is needed to understand why the children we identified who had spent lengthy periods in detention, had been forced to do so. We were told that the reasons for this include, but are not restricted to, attempts by the family to avert removal through further legal challenges. (2010, 6)

The report moves on to examine children's experiences of being arrested:

During our previous visit arrest had been the subject children complained about most consistently. To test whether children's experience of arrest had improved since then, and to evaluate subsequent changes to the *Enforcement Instructions and Guidance* (EIG)... children were given a series of statements concerning the arrest process and asked to say whether these were true or false. They were also given the opportunity to comment further on the issues these statements raised. (2010, 6)

Children were asked about their views and experiences:

We asked children whether the people who had brought them to Yarl's Wood were 'friendly and helpful'. Six agreed they were, while 10 disagreed. This finding echoed concerns raised in Yarl's Wood's children's forums that are chaired by their teachers. Children commented on the loud or violent way in which homes were entered, rude behaviour or treatment by officers, and the shadowing of children using the bathroom and toilet. Children also complained about being physically escorted from their homes, thereby making them feel and look like criminals. (2010)

The report concludes that

We stand by our contention that arrest and detention are inherently damaging to children, and that Yarl's Wood is no place for a child. While this does not mean that those with no entitlement should be allowed to stay, it does mean that attention must continue to be focused on the circumstances in which they are arrested and brought into detention, the process of detention itself and their removal and the conditions to which families return. (2010)

Reflection on research

This report is an inspection rather than research – although it shares many features with research, including a rigorous methodology.

Activity 1
How does the Children's Commissioner attempt to give a voice to children?

Activity 2
How do you feel about the way these children are being treated?

The moving account above helps us reflect further on this marginalized group of children. The experiences of such groups of displaced, unaccompanied and refugee children provide a very disturbing demonstration that globalization has a major impact on the worldwide experience of childhood. It has also challenged the role of the nation State – which is dealing directly with children from different parts of the world.

The eminent social theorist, Zygmunt Bauman (2003), has written of the consequences of globalization being the displacement of human beings who suffer the consequences of enormous global social change. Unaccompanied and refugee children are part of this process and are victims of this. But such children are also positive examples of children as agents of their own lives. Many have taken difficult decisions to take control of their own lives by travelling across boundaries and taking risks in order to improve their lives, or sometimes simply to survive violence and threats. As Mitchell (2007) has argued it is thus very important that they are not seen simply as 'problems', and that we understand 'what is happening when the problem is not happening' (Parton and O'Byrne, 2000, 56), by focusing on strengths as well as problems.

It is important to note that this is not a totally new challenge. For example, rather in reverse of the modern situation, England for many centuries practised sending its own children abroad. Child migrants, as they were known, were sent overseas by a range of organizations from the 1640s until the early 1960s. The stories of disjointed lives and fragmented identities have now been reconstructed by a number of commentaries (Bean and Melville, 1990). One key difference is that such children were unwittingly instruments of imperial and racial domination – today unaccompanied children come to a situation where they experience racism and discrimination.

Activities

Activity 1
We have seen some of the ways that children are transformed from passive 'objects' into active 'subjects'. Can you think of ways that children have become more active subjects during your life time?

Activity 2
When we look back at events, such as those in China outlined above, we can be surprised that these events ever happened. Can you think of ways that children are treated at the moment that might shock future generations?

Summary

This chapter has

- identified the way that children have been treated as objects in research, policy and practice;
- noted that children often actively resist the exercise of adult power;
- argued that children can be seen as active subjects, more and more in charge of their own lives;
- discussed how some groups of children who are marginalized face profound challenges in becoming active subjects.

Further reading

Archard, D. A. (2003) *Children, Family and the State*. Aldershot: Ashgate

This is an important book that explores many of the issues discussed in this book. It is a difficult read, but repays careful study.

Parton, N. (2006) *Safeguarding Childhood*. London: Palgrave

Parton develops his thinking in this book to take account of the growth of 'safeguarding' as a key organizing concept . The safeguarding idea went on to dominate English child welfare discourse.

Research details

Send down: a powerful State intervention

There can be few more powerful examples of the State intervening in the lives of children. The researchers explore the impact of a mass 'send down' from city to country on a generation of children.

Zhou, X. and Hou, L. (1999) 'Children of the Cultural revolution: the State and the Life Course in the People's Republic of China', *American Sociological Review*, 64, (1), 12–36

Giving children a voice in family decision-making

This research shows an example of children being given a real voice in family decision-making, when on the edge of State intervention. It demonstrates some of the challenges and how participation needs to be really worked at if it is to be effective for children.

Holland, S. and O'Neill, S. (2006) 'We had to be there to make sure it was what we wanted': Enabling children's participation in family decision-making through the family group conference', *Childhood*, 13, (1), 91–111

An international study of child well-being

The UNICEF study is one of the most significant pieces of research about children ever undertaken – both in terms of the international range and the impact it had when published. The study uses a number of dimensions to assess the 'well-being' of children, including children's subjective measure of their own well-being.

UNICEF (2007) 'Child poverty in perspective; an overview of child well-being in Rich Countries', *Innocenti Report Card no.7*. Florence

Children and participation in politics

This Welsh-based study examines the attitude of young people to political participation. The researchers find that while children express a general disinterest in politics they have a real interest in political issues that have an impact on their everyday lives.

Drakeford, M., Scourfield, J., Holland, S. and Davies, A., 'Welsh Children's Views On Government and Participation', *Childhood* 2009, 16, 247–264

Being a refugee or asylum seeker

Hek provides a valuable overview of research undertaken to explore the experiences of unaccompanied asylum seeking children and refugee children. The report provides valuable insights into the experiences of this marginalized group of children.

Hek, R. (2005) *The Experiences and Needs of Refugee and Asylum Seeking Children in the UK: A Literature Review*. Birmingham: University of Birmingham.

An Inspection of an Immigration Removal Centre by the Children's Commissioner for England

This is different from other examples of research utilized in this book as it is an inspection of a specific unit. However, it has much in common with research in terms of the methodological approach taken. The report is important in highlighting the challenges facing a marginalized group of children living in a difficult environment.

11 Million (2010) *The Children's Commissioner for England's follow up report to The Arrest and Detention of Children Subject to Immigration Control*. London: 11 Million

Being a Child in the Modern Family

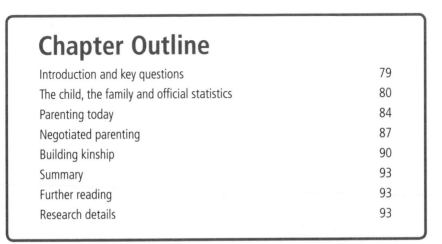

Chapter Outline

Introduction and key questions

Children experience two primary forms of adult power that has a direct impact on their lives. These are the power of parents and the power of professionals who work with children, and who are normally employed by the State. This chapter will explore the adult power that is exercised in families in the form of parenting and family decision-making.

The following questions will be addressed in this chapter:

What can official statistics tell us about family life?
How does parenting differ in style and what impact does this have on children?
How do families make key decisions in everyday life?
How do children view kinship relations?

The child, the family and official statistics

Anyone wishing to study childhood and the family has a rich source to draw on – the wealth of official statistics gathered by the State in order to inform government policy development. This chapter will use this official research data to develop our understanding of childhood and the family.

The official data on the family is extensive and informative. We can find out about a range of issues from how many people got married in a given year, to how many households own a refrigerator (www.ons.gov.uk). This data has many strengths – it is wide-ranging, draws on large samples (almost the whole population when the data is drawn from the census) and is largely reliable and informative. However, it would be a mistake to think that we could draw a totally accurate picture of childhood and families from the data. In this section we will provide some of the most useful data gathered by the Government, but we will also assess some of the problems, shortfalls and challenges present in the data.

One of the issues that often reaches the headlines of the newspapers is a perceived growth in the number of children born out of wedlock and an associated growth in the number of single parent families. These issues matter because they have very real effects on the everyday lives of people. For example, during the 2010 General Election in the United Kingdom, the Conservative Party based one of their key policies – the reintroduction of a married person's tax allowance – on the actual official statistics that are presented in Table 6.1. They argued that people had no incentive to get married and that this was increasing the number of children growing up outside of a stable family setting. When we look at the official statistics we can see some of the evidence supporting this argument.

Activity 1

Examine Table 6.1 – identify three trends that are suggested by the statistics.

Activity 2

In Activity 1 you may have identified some of the following trends:

- An increase in the number of one person households
- A decrease in the number of households with three or more children
- An increase in the number of lone parent households with dependent children

Table 6.1 Distribution of household types and structures, Great Britain, Social Trends (2000)

	1961	1971	1981	1991	2001
Type of household as a percentage of total					
One person	11	18	22	27	29
Two or more unrelated adults	5	4	5	3	2
One-family households					
Couple					
No Children	*26*	*27*	*26*	*28*	*30*
1–2 dependent children	*30*	*26*	*25*	*20*	*19*
3 + dependent children	*8*	*9*	*6*	*5*	*4*
Non- dependent children only	*10*	*8*	*8*	*8*	*6*
Lone parents					
Dependent children		*2*	*3*		
		5			
		6			
		7			
Non-dependent children only	*4*	*4*			
	4				
	4				
	3				
Multifamily households	3	1			
	1				
	1				
	1				
All households (millions)				16.3	
				18.6	
				20.2	
				22.4	

- The number of children born out of wedlock has increased throughout the period explored.
- This trend for children to be born out of wedlock increased significantly in the 1970s
- The trend for children to be born out of wedlock has steadied during the 1990s and 2000s

How can these changes be explained? An English government research paper suggests the following explanations:

- Changes in social norms reflect widespread acceptance of alternative family forms
- Legislation around family breakdown both reflects and drives changes in family composition and social norms

- Changes in women's employment and the availability of contraception have altered the timing of family formation
- People expect more romantic love and emotional closeness in relationships
- For most drivers, the effects are bidirectional and reinforcing e.g. changes in social norms are also the result of greater plurality in family forms (Cabinet Office, 2008, 22)

Thus far it may seem straightforward that the statistics suggest that evidence exists for the election policy mentioned above. However, there are a number of issues that the scholar of the family needs to address.

First, it is often the case that statistics tell us what is happening but they cannot really tell us why it is happening. A full picture also needs qualitative research to expand and explore the issues raised by the quantitative research outlined in the Table 6.1.

Second, official categories do not simply exist in the real world: for example, the definition of 'household' used by the government has changed over time. Barry Hindess has argued that official statistics are 'socially constructed' – that is the categories, measures and question asked have to be designed and the way that the statistics are gathered needs to be examined and explored:

> Official statistics must be analysed as a product. They are never mere givens to be taken as they are or else dismissed as inadequate. Like all products they must be examined in terms of the conditions of their production. (1973, 12)

Third, even if statistics are reliable and accurate to move from a statistic to a policy requires value-judgements and political calculations to be made. Statistics in themselves do not contain policies – the policies have to be built and derived from the statistics.

Thus we have seen there are at least three hurdles to jump before we move from statistics to policy. Smart reflects that debates on statistics have often been central:

> Much of the debate about the family in the late twentieth century has in fact been a struggle over the meaning of the statistics, with little attempt to refer to the admittedly limited research on the changes that have actually taken place inside family relationships, or to investigate them further. However, simple assertions as to the power of selfish individualism have had a significant effect on policy making on both sides of the Atlantic. (Smart, 2007, 14)

Let us examine these hurdles in terms of the statistics presented in Table 6.1.

First – we can tell what is happening; but why is it happening? This issue has been one of the great divides in what we have already stated, which the sociologists Berger and Berger identified as the 'war over the family'. We can read the statistics as signifying the decline of the traditional family, increased promiscuity and people putting their own needs before that of their children (see the work of Patricia Morgan and the *Daily Mail* columnist, Melanie Philips, who both argue these points). Or the very same statistics can be read as signs of more personal choice and freedom and a blossoming of alternative ways of raising children (see Fiona Williams, for example). In order to find out why social trends occur, the researcher will often want to undertake qualitative research – put simply this is research that asks the 'why' questions directly to a sample of people whose lives are reflected in the statistics. Williams and her colleagues asked people some of these why questions and uncovered what they called 'an ethic of care'. They found that people cared for each other and that they often had a strong sense of duty – but that this was not dependent on traditional ties of family and kinship. They often had strong ties of obligation to friends and the children of friends, for example. So while the decline of marriage may at first suggest people are becoming more individualistic and selfish when we explore lives in more depth this might not be the case.

Second, we need to explore the social construction of statistics (Hindess, 1973). In the example we have outlined, the official statistics ask people if they are married and uses this to assess the nature of their household. However, this is not a reliable measure. Thus, for example, someone completing a census form may state that they are married and this would be welcomed in some of the newspapers that worry about the decline of the family. But the marriage may be unhappy or even violent and perhaps the couple do not share a bedroom. In contrast an unmarried respondent to the census might be in a long-term, loving and caring relationship with the other parent – but would still count as a single parent in the official statistics. Thus the statistics can be misleading and we need in-depth, qualitative research to really grasp the reality of peoples' lives.

Finally, we argued above that moving from statistics to policy requires a number of political and moral decisions. Thus a feminist perspective might welcome the decline of the traditional family structure – this decline for a feminist might represent more freedom and choice for women and children. For the conservative commentator the very same statistic may represent a decline in family values, care and stability. Thus a statistic cannot speak for itself – it requires interpretation, judgement and action in order to become a social and political force.

Parenting today

During the early years of their lives most children are highly or totally dependent on their parent or parents. This dependency changes gradually until children enter their own transition to adulthood. Parenting itself is a complex and challenging process – it is demanding of the skills and values of parents and it has a high impact on children's social and psychological well-being.

The dominant research-based analysis of parenting styles is to see parenting falling into four main categories – indulgent, authoritarian, authoritative and uninvolved parenting. The example of research below summarizes a wide range of research that has been undertaken on parenting styles.

Example of research: parenting styles – a typology

Nancy Darling undertook an analysis of parenting style research, where she explored four types of parenting and the implications for children.

The researcher who seems to have first coined the phrase 'parenting style' was Diana Baumrind. The range of styles are designed to outline the normative range of parenting not taking into account the sort of parenting one might find in abusive or neglectful situations, for example. Baumrind argues that parenting style includes two key elements:

Parental responsiveness: which provides that element of parenting which is supportive and child orientated.

Parental demandingness: is that element of parenting which is aimed at actions which are aimed at integrating the child into existing situations.

Research suggests that there is a typology of four styles which contain different balances of demandingness and responsiveness. This typology is as follows:

Indulgent parents, who are sometimes referred to as permissive, and tend to allow self-regulation by the child and avoid confrontation. This typology is said to have two categories: permissive parents who proactively committed to their children and non-directive parents who lack this commitment.

Authoritarian parents tend to emphasize the demand side of parenting – they expect 'their orders to be obeyed without explanation' (Baumrind, 1991, 62).

Authoritative parents tend to balance both demanding and responsive elements: 'They want their children to be assertive as well as socially responsible and self-regulated as well as cooperative' (Baumrind, 1991, 62).

⇨

Uninvolved parents are low in both responsiveness and demandingness. At the extreme this style of parenting can become neglectful.

The proponents of a parenting styles typology argue that the style adopted has direct consequences for the child. Researchers have used parent interviews, child reports and observation and findings suggest that children who have experienced authoritative parenting feel they are more socially and 'instrumentally' competent. Children whose parents are uninvolved perform poorly in all the researched domains.

Researchers have tended to argue that authoritative parenting, 'is one of the most consistent family predictors of competence from early childhood through adolescence' (Darling, 1999, 2).

Reflections on the research

Activity 1
Which form of parenting to you feel that you experienced as a child?

Activity 2
If you are a parent, or may one day become a parent, which style of parenting would you aspire to adopt?

From the example of research box above we can see it is argued that there are four predominant, normative forms of parenting. Beyond these normative classifications a variation of this form of parenting was identified in one of the studies contributing to *Child Protection: Messages from Research* (1995) as abusive. This form of parenting was known as 'low warmth/high criticism' and generates low self-esteem for the child and is therefore effectively neglectful.

Outside of this 'parenting styles' framework the sociologist Anthony Giddens has developed the idea of the 'democratic family'. Giddens places this with the framework of modernity and contemporary childhood and writes from a sociological perspective rather than the psychological tradition utilized by parenting styles researchers.

Giddens' work is theoretical in nature – he has observed wider social trends but has not undertaken detailed fieldwork about how families work. However, such research has been undertaken by researchers exploring the nature of decision-making in families. One such project is considered in the example of research box below.

Research example: Involvement of children in family decision-making

Butler et al. (2005) undertook research funded by the Joseph Rowntree Foundation on how children were involved in family-based decision-making in England.

> The researchers undertook group interviews with 69 children and interviews with another 48, all the children were aged 8 to 11. They found that decision-making was usually informal – there were few explicit or formal rules. These decision-making processes were found to be democratic, which applied to major decisions such as when to move house. One 11-year-old girl stated, 'all of us decided to move 'cos we didn't like where we were staying'. (2005, 2).

Some decision-making was conditional – for example, it was dependent on the children being seen as 'good'. The researchers argue that

> the cumulative, implicit and subtle processes for family decision-making would seem to rely on a shared and intimate knowledge of the family's habits and customary practices as well as on a degree of mutual trust. (2005, 2)
>
> Parental authority seems to arise from competence – which can be questioned by children when they feel more competent than their parents. Children had a strong sense of 'fairness' – where 'having a say' was more important than necessarily 'getting their own way', 'Fairness, for most children, meant being able to be part of the 'democracy' of the family'. (2005, 2).

Children's sense of private space was important – 'children were prepared to risk confrontation and friction and even sometimes lie to parents' – in relation to issues such as bedrooms.

Most children thought their competence to make their own decisions would increase with age. Children thought that parents were usually in agreement with each other on decisions. But mothers were most frequently consulted in relation to domestic factors. Fathers became involved in bigger decisions, such as holidays or moving house.

The researchers suggest that there are the following implications of their research for those providing services:

> understand and respect the complexity of family processes, family histories and the particular ways that families have of going about their everyday business;
>
> Respect the authority of parents, the confidence that many children have in their parents and the capacity of children to engage meaningfully and purposefully in determining the conduct of family life;
>
> Respect children's inclination towards participatory forms of engagement in family life and be sensitive to children who are in the process of developing their capacity for autonomy and independence;
>
> Respect and respond to children's claims to fairness and equitable treatment (2005, 4)

⇨

Reflections on the research

This research helps us to reflect on the everyday and in a sense 'mundane' ways that families work in their day-to-day lives.

Activity 1
How would you describe the nature of decision-making during your childhood?

Activity 2
If you are a parent, or may become one, which style of decision-making would you aspire to adopt in your family?

Negotiated parenting

While much of this book has been concerned with large-scale social and political concerns it is a healthy reminder that childhood actually exists in a mundane day-to-day sense of decisions about food, bedtimes and going out. Parenting is a nuanced and complex process requiring careful thought and a series of delicately balanced decisions, these themes are explored further in the Research examples below.

Example of research: parental supervision of children

The researchers interviewed 50 young people and one or both of their parents – the participants also self-completed a seven-day diary. Both parents and young people understood monitoring and supervision to mean that parents would know where young people were and what they were doing, so that they could ensure that young people were safe. Part of this was being aware of a young person's emotional well-being as well as the more obvious physical safety.

For parents this process involved setting boundaries and establishing rules. How this framework actually worked depended partly on the nature and quality of communication between parent and child.

New technology was significant here – most of the young people had a mobile phone. The phone could be used to inform parents of changes of plan or if problems had emerged. Parents were concerned about the dangers arising from use of the internet.

The burden of the monitoring of childhood fell mainly to mothers and, thus, young people reported feeling more comfortable talking to their mothers. Monitoring also involved wider networks – networks which included extended family, friends and schools.

⇨

The factors that were influential in terms of the nature of the supervision adopted included factors such as neighbourhood, age, gender and individual personality. The researchers state that

> Young people, therefore, were aware of the impact of their relationships with their parents had on their behaviour, and knew what their parents would consider as acceptable or unacceptable behaviour. (2005, 2)

The researchers conclude that

> this research has shown that parents generally take monitoring and supervision seriously and consider it to be an important part of their care and protection of children. It is a complex process that involves parents, young people and a wider support network, and is dependent on the quality of the parent-child relationship. (2005, 4)

In the United Kingdom, the Labour government (1997–2010) was particularly interested in how parents supervised young people and what role the State could play in this. The researchers suggest that their finding could be utilized to inform parenting programmes and the admission of Parenting Orders.

Reflections on the research

We can see here how some everyday, but nevertheless complex decisions are taken within families.

Activity 1
How was your activity monitored during your childhood? How intensive was any monitoring?

Activity 2
How has the monitoring of childhood changed since you were a child? What factors have contributed to any changes?

We can see how complex being a parent and being a child is in the contemporary world. The world is changing rapidly – the leading commentator Zygmunt Bauman often uses the word 'liquid' to describe the modern world and the pace of change (Bauman, 2007). Parents and children have to respond quickly and creatively to these changes – making it very difficult to be a parent or child, and to negotiate what it means to be a family. Beck Gernsheim quotes Kaufmann et al. in reflecting on these complex challenges:

> In advanced industrial society, then, the physical care of children has in many respects become easier, thanks to the introduction of technology into the home

and the availability of such products as disposable nappies or convenience baby-food. But, on the other hand, the modern discovery of childhood has brought with it new aspects and tasks which place growing demands upon parents. As one large-scale study of the family concluded, 'the norm of the ethical and social responsibility of parents is reaching 'a historically unprecedented level'. (Kaufmann et al., 1984 in Beck Gernsheim, 2002, 90)

Our next example of research explores the underpinning nature of what provides the material basis for effective parenting. Again we will find that this a delicate, negotiated process.

Example of research: what is essential for family life?

The English Department for Work and Pensions commissioned research into what parents regarded as necessities for their children. Work such as this helps to underpin government decision-making about benefit levels and policy.

The study convened groups of parents, 45 participants in total, to ask them:

> to identify specific items that could be classified as necessities for families with children, and whose absence is likely to cause hardship to families unable to afford them. (Hirsch and Smith, 2010, 2)

The researchers found that parents prioritize

> necessities that affect social relationships within families. For example, they think that a family home should have an area where the family can eat together. (2010, 2)

This includes family outings and short holidays.

> Health and well-being were also regarded as essential – including a healthy, varied diet and opportunities to exercise – for example, riding a bicycle.
>
> Parents felt that some essential activities should be socially subsidized to ensure that families could participate.
>
> Judgements about information and communication technologies 'are in a state of transition' (2010, 2), but most felt that a computer was now essential for family life.

The researchers argue that they have built an understanding of what makes a 'socially perceived necessity' in Britain today.

Reflections on research

This work helps us reflect on the underpinning material factors that make up family life, and how this is perceived by parents. Children were not asked about their views as part of this project.

⇨

Activity 1
What do you consider to be a necessity in a modern Western society? How might children's views differ from adult perspectives?

Activity 2
Would you agree that resources that promote 'social relationships' are important for families to work well?

Again we can see how many complex decisions make up the day-to-day reality of parenting and childhood.

Building kinship

Our next example helps us understand how children, perhaps more fundamentally, can actively contribute to the understanding of what actually makes up family and kinship networks. Here the focus is powerfully on children as active subjects.

Example of research: making your own family network

This study by Mason and Tipper is important in developing the concept of family practices by examining how children actually construct their own family and kinship networks:

> The study was designed to explore practices, perceptions and experiences involved in children's kinship. (2008, 442)

The following methodology was adopted by the researchers:

> We conducted qualitative interviews with 49 children aged 7–12, from a range of socioeconomic, cultural and ethnic backgrounds also gave the children a disposable camera prior to the interview, and asked them to take photographs of 'who mattered' to them, or of places and things that they associated with who mattered. These photographs were then used in a process of 'photo-elicitation' in interview discussions with the children about who was significant in their lives and how they defined and experienced kinship. Most children also completed a 'concentric circles' map, which plotted their emotional closeness or distance to people they talked to us about, and some also chose to do drawings of their family or relatives. (2008, 442–443)

⇨

When identifying one of the key themes of this book complexity emerges as a defining issue:

> although our study did not seek out children who had experienced dramatic family change, almost all had relationships with kin that might be considered 'unconventional' or complex, or which required children to think beyond conventional genealogical definitions based, for example, on heterosexual marriage, nuclear families or kinship based on a single cultural model. In fact, we would argue that this is the *ordinary complexity of kinship*, for both children and adults. (2008, 443)

The researchers argue that five ways of 'reckoning kinship' by children emerge from their findings:

> Acknowledging 'proper' relations
> Creating enhanced kinship with 'proper' relatives
> Establishing distance from 'proper' relatives
> Weighing up potential 'proper' relatives
> Creating like-family kinship

The role of children as active subjects emerges from the study:

> we have also been keen to establish that the children in our study exercised considerable creativity in defining their own kinship and in making sense of it. Of course, given that kinship is constructed relationally, between people, the creativity of children influences the shape and experience of kinship for adults too. (2008, 457)

The researchers argue that

> To begin with, cultural constructions of childhood, and of adult–child relationships and responsibilities, are likely to form an important backdrop for the negotiation of children's kinship, although we do not think they determine the 'outcomes'. There is a sense from our data that the children in our study are comfortable to an extent with the idea that they have some licence to, for example, say someone is like family, or to resist adult interpretations or indeed to distance 'proper' kin…this 'licence' is more readily possible in a socio-legal and cultural context where there is some (however ambiguous) acceptance of the idea of children's participation, or that the interests and perspectives of the child might not entirely reflect those of adults…We also think that public understandings and legal definitions of what constitutes relatedness, kinship or family are significant, and to the extent that these vary culturally and nationally, they will provide a different formal backdrop to children's kinship. (2008, 458)
>
> We hope that the idea of modes of reckoning may be useful and applicable across a range of cultures and contexts. Children in different situations may start with different formal frameworks, or contexts, for defining 'proper' relatives, but kinship may still be enhanced, distanced or created, and how this

⇨

works in different contexts seems to us to be an empirical question worthy of further exploration. (2008, 458)

Reflections on the research

This study has expanded our idea of family practices and examined how this actually works in day-to-day settings. The perspectives of children are absolutely central to this research project.

Activity 1
Think about your family and kinship network. What is particular about it – for example, do you call someone Aunt who is not biologically an aunt, is someone treated like a family member even though they strictly are not a family member?

Activity 2
Can you think about any other further research in this area, which Mason and Tipper suggest may be required?

In this important study we see how children can be seen as active in how kinship is defined and negotiated. This is an example of children actively making their own world, which is a long way from the passive children constructed by developmental psychology or in official statistics.

Activities

The following activities are designed to help reflect back on some of the key concerns over the chapter as a whole.

Activity 1
Think about your own family and kinship network. How has this family changed in recent years? Do any of these changes reflect wider social changes in family and household structures discussed in this chapter?

Activity 2
How do you evaluate recent changes in people's lifestyles? What do you regard as positive ? Are there any of the trends discussed in this chapter that concern you? If so why?

Summary

This chapter has

- examined what it means to be a family and how the complexities of everyday life are negotiated
- explored how official statistics are useful, but need to be interpreted carefully
- reported research that suggests there are four potential parenting styles
- discovered how families have to make complex decisions about issues like supervision and material resources
- pointed out how children have active views on how family and kinship are constituted

Further reading

Cabinet Office/Department of Children, Schools and Families (2008) *Families in Britain: An Evidence Paper*. London

A very useful paper – which is full of relevant data and diagrammatic representations. The paper is particularly interesting as it is an official document that is clearly underpinned by a family practices approach.

Research details

Official statistics and families

The government produces a considerable amount of research relevant to this book. It is not only important to study and understand this data, but also to read it critically.

Distribution of household types and structures, Great Britain, Social Trends (2000), London, HMSO

Parenting styles – a typology

This underpinning analysis of parenting styles is utilized extensively to understand parenting. The four types are useful in helping us understand the differing ways that parents relate to children.

Darling, N. (1999) 'Parenting style and its correlates'. *ERIC Digest*, EDO-PS-99–3

Parental supervision of children

The way that parents and children negotiate around issues of control and supervision are essential to understanding the everyday nuances of parenting.

Stace, S. and Roker, D. (2005) *Parental Supervision: The Views and Experiences of Young People and Their Parents*. York: JRF Findings

Involvement of children in family decision-making

This study researched how children aged between 8 and 11 are involved in everyday decision-making in families.

Butler, I., Robinson, M. and Scanlan, L. (2005) *Children and Decision-Making*. National Children's Bureau: London

What is essential for family life?

Family life is underpinned by material concerns about the basics that are required for families to undertake a successful family life. This study explores how decisions are made and what people regard as essential for family life.

Hirsch, D. and Smith, N. (2010) 'Family values – parents' views on necessities for families with children', *Research Report 641*, London: Department for Work and Families

Making your own family network

Mason and Tipper explore children as active subjects in 'reckoning' family and kinship. It demonstrates how complex family life is and how children contribute actively to the processes of family life.

Mason, J. and Tipper, B. 'Being Related: How children define and create kinship', *Childhood*, 15, (4), 441–460

Being a Child of the State

Introduction and key questions

As we have seen earlier there is one group of children who have what we might call an 'enhanced' or 'developed' relationship with the State – they are children in care. This group of children are cared for by the State and the State can often hold 'parental responsibility' for them. These children may have well have experienced a problematic relationship with their birth family. Children in care therefore are central to the concerns of this book, and they have a particular interest in the triangle of childhood, families and the State.

This group of children have, in some countries, travelled a journey that can be compared to children more widely – a journey of being treated as passive, and often institutionalized, recipients of services where they have become recognized as active participants in their own lives. We are now aware that many of these children will have suffered forms of physical, sexual and psychological abuse while in the care system an issue that will be particularly explored in this chapter.

In this chapter we will examine the following questions:

What is the relationship between children in care and the State?
How well does the State look after the children it cares for?
Why are these children sometimes abused by those who are supposed to care for them?
How can the system better protect these children and improve their life chances?
How can children in care be active participants in their own lives?

Children in care

Children in care live in an 'enhanced' relationship with the State. In terms of our triangle their relationship with family would often be weakened or troubled, and their direct relationship with the State would be stronger than with the majority of children. Legally, in many jurisdictions, the State is the parent of the child – these children are, quite literally, 'children of the State'.

Three main themes emerge from a historical analysis undertaken by the author of child welfare provision for children who are separated from their parents in the United Kingdom.

These three themes are

First, the long shadow of the Poor Law, which made the provision that state welfare should be 'less eligible' or, in everyday words, of a lower standard than life in the community, has been influential in terms of the stigma associated with being 'in care'. Second, there has historically been an emphasis on education and training as methods of rescuing children from poverty, or from what we would now perceive as 'poor outcomes'. Finally, there have been tensions between family based care (fostering and adoption) and residential provision for children. (Frost and Parton, 2009, 96)

This analysis raises three key questions:

(a) Can children be 'children of the State' without carrying a stigma or disadvantage?
(b) Can the State deliver positive outcomes for children in care?
(c) How can the tensions between family-based care and institutional care be delivered?

First of all we will examine a fundamental, and perhaps emblematic, issue in terms of children in care: the abuse of children in care.

Understanding abuse in the care system

While the care system has many successes, and works well for many children (Stein, 2006b), one of the persistent challenges of the system is why members of staff who are asked to look after children sometimes abuse them? It is now proven that the physical and sexual abuse of children in care took place and that examples can be found in all corners of the planet (see, for example, Waterhouse, 2000, Young, 2008).

Here we provide an example of the persistent and extensive abuse of children, a narrative that could be repeated in many corners of the globe.

Example of research/inquiry: an example of widespread abuse

For many years throughout the latter half of the twentieth century it was known that there had been extensive abuse of children in care in North Wales. After many legal complications and delays eventually a full and comprehensive report was produced – the report of the inquiry was chaired by Ronald Waterhouse and entitled *Lost in Care* (2000). The lengthy report considered and edited a considerable amount of material, including evidence from 575 witnesses. Waterhouse summarized the scale of the challenge as follows:

> It had been known for several years that serious sexual and physical abuse had taken place in homes managed by Clwyd County Council in the 1970s and 1980s. A major police investigation had been begun in 1991, resulting in 8 prosecutions and 6 convictions of former care workers, but speculation that the actual abuse had been greater in scale had persisted in North Wales. (2000, 2.01)

The report outlines the severe and persistent abuse of children and young people over a number of decades. To give a flavour of the many hundreds of pages presented by Waterhouse we present below just one of incidents reported to give us a sense of both the extent and the seriousness of the abuse:

> The allegations of sexual abuse by (a member of staff) Howarth span the whole of his period at Bryn Estyn (from November 1973) to July 1984. They

⇨

---

were centred mainly on the flat that he occupied there on the first floor of the main building. It was Howarth's practice to invite boys, usually five or six from the main building at a time, to the flat in the evening for drinks and light food: they would watch television and play cards or board games. Invitations to these sessions were by a 'flat list' complied by Howarth or made up on his instructions and boys who went to the flat were required to wear pyjamas without underpants…Howarth was tried in July 1994 in Chester Crown Court on 3 counts of buggery and 9 of indecent assault. These offences were alleged to have been committed between 1 Jan 1974 and 11 May 1984 and they involved 9 boy residents…he was convicted on 8 July 1994 of one offence of buggery and 7 indecent assaults, for which he was sentenced to 10 years' imprisonment. (2000: 8 April 2007)

Graphic and disturbing accounts such as this are to be found across the numerous pages of the Waterhouse Report. The Report concludes as follows:

widespread shortcomings in practice and administrative failings in the provision of children's services, including failure to apply basic safeguards provided for by regulation, which must be addressed by local authorities are to discharge adequately the parental responsibilities imposed upon them in respect of looked after children. The Children Act 1989 has provided a springboard for many improvements in children's services but the need for vigilance and further positive action remains if the ever present risk of abuse is to be minimised. (2000, 55.09)

Reflections on the research/inquiry

Activity 1
Apply the Wardlaugh and Wilding framework (in the example of research box below) to the data provided above by Waterhouse. Does it provide a convincing explanatory framework?

Activity 2
Why does the abuse of children in institutions often go overlooked for many years?

This report provides us with an officially verified overview of a widespread, disturbing and challenging social problem. We have many reports and inquiries, in addition to court cases and convictions, which provide an eloquent, trustworthy and moving testament.

This issue had a high profile and was in danger of bringing the entire system of children's social care, in particular residential care, into disrepute, rather in the way that similar challenges faced the Roman Catholic church as allegations emerged early in the twenty-firstt century, some of which did occur in residential settings.

The reports and the eloquent testimony of children across the globe certainly reflected a crisis in the care system. These tragic events raise many issues that are the concern of this book. The events clearly present an extreme example of the abuse of adult power over children. They demonstrate the serious consequences of children being silenced, of being invisible and of not being treated as full human beings.

The extent of abuse within the system tends to reinforce the first historical theme we examined earlier that residential care is stigmatized and 'less eligible'. How can abuse such as this be explained? The box below explores one attempt to provide an explanation.

Example of research: why does abuse occur in care settings?

The researchers studied official inquires into the abuse of children in State care by care staff. Having studied the reports the researchers provide the following eight propositions which propose an attempt to explain what they conceptualize as 'the corruption of care'.

The eight points they propose to explain abuse in care are as follows:

- The corruption of care depends on the neutralization of normal moral concerns.
- The corruption of care is closely connected with the balance of power and powerlessness in organizations.
- Particular pressures and particular kinds of work are associated with corruption of care.
- Management failure underlies the corruption of care.
- The corruption of care is more likely in enclosed, inward looking organizations.
- The absence of clear lines and mechanisms of accountability plays an important part in the corruption of care.
- Particular models of work and organizations are conducive to the corruption of care.
- The nature of certain client groups encourages the corruption of care.

Reflections on the research

Activity 1
How convincing do you find the researcher's explanations of abuse in care?

Activity 2
What can be done to reverse and challenge the factors identified by the researchers?

⇨

We can see from official reports that abuse in care has been extensive and difficult for policy makers to address. The theoretical perspective offered by Wardhaugh and Wilding (1993) suggests that such abuse has different dimensions and is multi-causal. Policy to address abuse in care needs to address these fundamental challenges.

What emerges powerfully from the literature on abuse in care is the key theme of the abuse of adult power over vulnerable children and young people. There are extreme forms of power differentials between children in care and those who are supposed to care for them. Where such power is deployed and exploited the results are profound and damaging.

Judith Ennew (1986), in her classic analysis of global child sexual exploitation, demonstrates how sexual abuse occurs where there are the most extreme disparities in power. She argues using the example of global sexual exploitation how mainly rich, white, Western adult males exploit mainly poor, black, developing world, female children: the disparity of power is demonstrated in each aspect of this relationship. As the American researcher of child abuse, David Finkelhor, argues cogently, 'abuse tends to gravitate towards the relationships of greatest power differential' (1986, 18). All adult relationships tend to be mediated through the unequal use of power – the misuse of this power can be seen wherever child abuse takes place.

Children in care add another dimension of powerlessness, a dimension not mentioned by Ennew. Without the protection that can be offered by family, often labelled as 'damaged', and living in situations such children are vulnerable to the abuse of power in the ways that were outlined, for example, in the Waterhouse Report (2000).

Here we have examined just one aspect of the disadvantage facing children in care and one root of the stigma that often attaches itself to those in care: alternatively we could have examined issues such as education or health. Does this suggest that the State can never deliver positive outcomes for children it cares for?

The challenge of outcomes

The second historical theme mentioned in introducing this chapter was the issue of outcomes and whether care can improve outcomes for children of the State. It is often assumed, and is almost part of 'common sense' and 'folk wisdom', that the care system is bound to fail the children it looks after. This then becomes closely related to the issue of stigma that we have already mentioned. Stein in the example of research below challenges this perspective.

Example of research – can the State deliver for the children it looks after?

Stein (2006b) has produced a telling and influential critique of this basic assumption that the outcomes for children in care are overwhelmingly and necessarily poor. Stein argues that

> the political and professional consensus that the care system is to blame for society's woes is wrong.

Stein draws on an extensive body of research and gives five reasons for this argument which will be summarized below.

First, many young people only spend a brief period in State care and thus this cannot be expected to have any significant impact on outcomes.

Second, many of those who leave State care between the ages of 16–18, come into care between 10–15, often from disadvantaged family backgrounds, and they may well have already disrupted educational experiences. Stein argues that to expect any significant impact in outcomes for this group is again flawed.

Third, Stein argues that we need to distinguish between three groups of care leavers. First, those who 'move on' from State care and who often have successful outcomes. Second there are those who 'survive' and may do well if they are adequately supported. Finally Stein argues that there is a group who are highly vulnerable, and who form perhaps 5 per cent of the total care population, but who are strongly associated with a 'failing' care system.

Fourth, outcomes may well improve as young people become older – having come through the usual challenges experienced by all of us in terms of youth transitions. More longitudinal research work is required to explore these issues.

Fifth, and finally, current outcome measures are too crude as they tend to detach the young people from their backgrounds and thus fail to take into account their starting points.

Stein concludes that what we actually need is a progress measure that would be more realistic than regarding State care as necessarily negative. Stein argues that it is unrealistic to expect the care system to compensate for wider social problems and challenges, as if it existed in isolation.

As we have seen above Stein argues that the State can deliver positives outcomes for children in care, and points out some of the ways in which this might be facilitated in happening (see also Stein, 2009).

Family care or institutional care?

Having examined stigma and outcomes the third theme emerging from our initial historical review is the tension between family-based provision and institutional or residential care. These questions again are at the heart of the concerns of the book.

Some have argued that where family has failed then the State should try to reproduce the family. This can be carried out in three forms:

(a) Kinship care – where carers are found for the child within the extended family and kinship network
(b) Foster care – where children live with 'strangers' who offer a family living environment, without taking legal guardianship
(c) Adoption – where a new parent or parents take permanent legal responsibility for a child.

All these three are forms of substitute family care where the State intervenes to try to reproduce family life for the child (see Frost, Mills and Stein, 1999).

The alternative is to provide a form of care in some sort of children's home. Across the globe these vary between units which care for a small number of children, to large institutions that may house hundreds of children. Whilst aiming to be caring and nurturing these institutions do not aim to reproduce the family, but rather to substitute for it.

Taking control? The lives of children in care

How can the challenges of the care system be addressed? Can children in care be empowered to take more control over their own lives? Below we provide two examples of research – one of which demonstrates how children in care are sometimes denied control over their own lives, and then a more optimistic example demonstrating 'what makes the difference'.

Example of research: being excluded from decision-making

Leeson reflects on how

> the extent to which young people are involved in legal decision-making depends on assumptions and perceptions about their ability to participate in decision-making in general. (Leeson, 2007, 268)

She has undertaken in-depth, qualitative research with four young people who have experience of care:

> four young people aged between 12 and 14 years, were asked to recall and analyse their experiences through interviews, games and craft experiences. (2007, 268)

She argues that the following themes emerge from her research:

> The overwhelming feelings of helplessness experienced as a consequence of not being involved in decision-making and the serious impact this had on their future (2007, 272)
> The experience of corporate parenting as impersonal and system oriented, not child centred (2007, 273)
> The importance of having staff who were consistent, concerned and worked as advocates on behalf of the child (2007, 273)
> That attempts to communicate their feelings had met with a lack of understanding from key adults, as the methods the boys had used had apparently not been recognised or had been misconstrued (2007, 273)

Leeson concludes that the care system needs to address

> the importance of involvement in decision-making
> the challenge to adult assumptions about childhood and competency
> the importance of listening to children

The article concludes with the words of one of the children:

> we need real choices, we need time to think and we need people who are prepared to listen and help. (2007, 276)

Reflections on the research

This research is one of many that reflect on children in care who are often disempowered – sometimes by acts of omission or commission by members of staff, and perhaps more often by elements of the care system that operate to deny them power over their own lives

⇨

Activity 1

How does the care system operate to reduce the opportunities for children to take control of their own lives? Why might this be different from family-based context?

Activity 2

How can children in care be given more power and control over their own lives?

The example of research above clearly demonstrates how children in care can sometimes be treated in ways that makes them feel excluded from key processes that have a major impact on their own lives. Below we explore a more optimistic example that demonstrates that the care system can be empowering and positive.

Example of research: empowering young people in care

This research undertaken by the Rainer organization provides a good example of young people being empowered as researchers and suggests a positive framework for the care experience, utilizing the phrase 'what makes the difference'.

The research team explains the process as follows:

> This peer research has provided an opportunity for young people from care to find out from 265 of their peers, from across England, 'what made the difference' for them. It also provided a valuable learning experience for the 33 young people who were trained as part of this work and for the local authorities who supported them, and stands as a good example to others of how to empower young people, for whom we are corporate parents, to play their role in improving outcomes. The results of our work stand as testimony to the young people's knowledge, enthusiasm, determination and ability. Perhaps in addition, their work illustrates that in our struggle to improve outcomes for young people from care we often ignore their role as key partners in our task. (2007, 13)

Young people were prepared to undertake the research:

> Care experienced young people were trained to interview young people in their own local authorities to ascertain young people's views, opinions and experiences. Thirty-three young people were trained from 25 local authorities to complete the 265 interviews across England. (2007, 6)

The sample of young people interviewed was as follows:

> In late 2006, face-to-face interviews were conducted with 265 young people, aged between 15and 23, from 25 local authority areas. Roughly

⇨

equal proportions of the interviewees were young men and young women. The majority were white, reflecting the ethnic makeup of the care population. About one in seven was disabled and one in five was a parent. Three-quarters had left care, two-thirds of these before reaching the age of 18. (2007, 6)

The questions asked focused on a connecting theme: 'what makes the difference'.

The key findings are outlined below. First of all what made the difference in terms of accommodation?

- Support from family/friends and carers
- The quality of support
- Feeling independent
- Choice and control
- Education and financial support (2007, 7)

Next what made the difference in terms of preparation and planning?

> Many felt what was essential was the availability of flexible, responsive advice – knowing that at least one key person was there for them, checking on them regularly. (2007, 7)

The report then explores, what made the difference in terms of education?

Advice and information
Help in choosing or accessing courses or training
Help to focus on what to do in life
Encouragement, support and motivation
Encouragement or being made to go to school
Help with homework
Practical help – being provided with a computer
Work and volunteering experience
Positive attitudes from carers and workers (2007, 8)

In more overall terms respondents were asked 'what makes the difference' to their care experience:

Safety
Relationships with family
Positive, caring relationships with others
Help with leaving care
Becoming a parent (2007, 11)

The respondents were then asked what was the best thing about the care experience? They replied:

Feeling emotionally secure and supported
Feeling safe
Opportunities for fun and enjoyment
Opportunities for self-development

⇨

Financial and material support
New friendships, bonds and social skills (2007, 11)

The respondents were then asked what one thing could have made care better for them? Their responses were as follows:

Quality of care/more emotional support and understanding from people who genuinely care
Stability of placements and people
Feeling part of a family
Being listened to
Financial and practical help (2007, 11)

The report summarizes the findings as follows:

Getting into care was appreciated and a positive experience for many, especially being removed from previously negative experiences. It was clear that the amount of contact young people wanted with their natural families was an individual issue, over which they would like to exercise more choice. Relationships with family beyond parents, especially siblings, grandparents, aunts and uncles, were a valued source of support. Experiencing good quality support; positive, sincere, caring relationships; help with psychological issues; and being able to feel emotionally secure, supported and safe. No one type of professional stood out more positively or negatively than others: each young person's experience had varied in relation to whom they felt had provided them with the right support, including family and friends. Choice, control, quality and becoming independent were the critical factors in relation to their placements and accommodation. Many of the young people really appreciated the encouragement and support they had had with education and self-development, and the chance to experience family life and opportunities, which they felt they would not have done otherwise. (2007,12)

Reflections on the research

This research contrasts with the previous 'example of research' box where negative experiences of being parented by the State were explored. Here we see young people empowered as researchers and focusing on the positive take of 'what makes the difference'?

Activity 1
Why is it important that young people were empowered to undertake their own research, with support from adults?

Activity 2
The research report suggests how life in care can be improved. What are the barriers to ensuring that these changes happen?

Children in care in the wider context

As we have argued throughout this book childhood is best seen as living a range of rich and diverse childhoods: so it is with children in care. As a result the factors of gender, ethnicity, disability and social class, alongside the particular and specific care experiences, are crucial to understanding children in care. As a result when we discuss children in care we need to place these debates in the wider context of debates about difference and diversity. As a result it is not possible to separate being a child in care from being a childhood in the wider social context. As has been argued elsewhere:

> The care system always bears a relationship to wider social and political themes – we cannot understand the care system without relating it to issues of social class, gender, disability and ethnicity, for example. (Frost, Mills and Stein, 1999, 25)

Children in care in many ways act as a proxy for wider social problems. An increase in child abuse, an increase in pressure on the family or a growth of poverty and inequality are all likely to lead to an increase in the number of children in care.

In reality we cannot expect the care system to act as a solution when issues in our State, family, childhood triangle start to go wrong. The care system indeed acts more as a safety net for children who the wider social system has let down. Thus an understanding of the care system must be located in a wider debate about contemporary childhood that we have explored throughout this book.

Activities

The following activities are designed to help reflect back on some of the key concerns over the chapter as a whole.

Activity 1
We have seen some of the challenges facing children in care. What can be done to improve the lives of children in care?

Activity 2
Do you think that children in care might still be abused in care? Can we ensure that abuse in care will never re-occur?

Summary

This chapter has

examined the lives of children in care

explored the nature of abuse in care and how this might be explained

analysed the outcomes for children in care and discussed whether current outcome
measures are sufficient

demonstrated how children can become active subjects within the care system

Further reading

Frost, N. and Parton, N. (2009) *Understanding Children's Social Care.* London: Sage

This book utilizes research, theory and policy analysis to understand State intervention in childhood.

Stein. M. (2009) *Quality Protects.* London: Jessica Kingsley Press

This book provides a readable summary of a wide range of research studies that explore how the State works with 'children in need' and children in care. It provides a range of useful policy and practice guidance.

Research details

An example of widespread abuse

This is probably the most wide-ranging study of abuse in a given geographical region. Waterhouse heard the voice of children, albeit years after their abuse had taken place and reconstructed an extensive and moving account of abuse across a network of institutionalized settings.

Waterhouse, R. (2000) *Lost in Care: Summary of Report.* London: Stationery Office.

Why does abuse occur in care settings?

This is a theoretical paper drawing on a wide range of inquiry and research evidence. The authors provide a useful theoretical framework for understanding abuse in care settings.

Wardhaugh, J. and Wilding, P. (1993) 'Towards an explanation of the corruption of care', *Critical Social Policy*, 37, 4–31

Can the State deliver for the children it looks after?

This short article provides a brief and excellently written summary of the authors numerous research studies. Stein argues that the predominant mood of pessimism about the outcomes of the care system could be misplaced. The article argues for more nuanced measures of outcomes that can measure 'valued-added' rather than crude outcomes.

Stein. M, (2006b), 'A wrong turn?', *Guardian*, 6 January 2006

Being excluded from decision-making

This small-scale study is significant in using innovative and child-centred research methods to give a voice to children in care. The research helps us to understand how large the task is in terms of making State care a positive experience for all.

Leeson, C. (2007) 'My life in care: experiences of non-participation in decision-making processes in decision-making processes', *Child & Family Social Work*, 12, (3), 268–277

Empowering young people in care

This research suggests how the State can make an effective parent for children in care. It focuses on the question 'what makes the difference'. The study provides us with a good example of how children can be empowered to undertake their own research on issues that matter to them.

Rainer (2007) *What Makes the Difference*. London: WMTD/Rainer and NCB

8 Reinventing the Relationship between Childhood, Families and the State

Introduction and key questions

How can we summarize the main arguments and themes of this book?

First, we have seen that our three main concerns – children, families and the State – are complex and varied. They all resist an easy definition or fixed understanding.

Second, all three exist in a complex interaction with each other. They all have an impact on each other and they interact with each other. No single one of these social institutions – childhood, families or the State – can be understood in isolation from the other.

Third, change is a part of all three social institutions. None of them stand still – they are all dynamic, fluid and always changing. It follows that our thinking, our theories and our practices have to be equally fluid and responsive to the complex changes taking place with the triangular relationship.

Fourth, we have seen how, in many arenas, children are emerging from the shadows – of history, research, policy and politics (Jones, 2009). But we should not assume that this is inevitable or will always travel in one direction – children and their advocates will suffer setbacks and defeats in their struggle to have a voice and to be taken seriously. Riley (1983), for example, provides an excellent example of how policy towards children changed very rapidly at the end of the Second World War.

Having summarized our main themes we will now utilize the research and theory we have explored in an attempt to answer the following (rather ambitious) questions:

How can we reinvent the relationship between children and families?
How can we reinvent the relationship between children and the State?

Rethinking children and families

We have seen how complex the place of the child is within diverse family structures and we have noted how family practices are fluid, changing and being constantly reinvented. David Morgan argues that the notion of

'family practices' was elaborated to convey a sense of flow and movement between a whole set of overlapping social practices, practices which were both constructed by the observer and lived by the actual practitioners. Thus 'family', in this account, is not a thing but a way of looking at, and describing, practices which might also be described in a variety of other ways. (1996, 199)

The new dominance of this way of thinking can be seen in the following quote from a British government publication:

For the purpose of this paper we **define** family by what families do (functional definition) rather than by a particular form or legal structure. The paper postulates that everybody is part of a family at some time in their lives and what family is and does depends on the particular life-stage of an individual. (Cabinet Office, 2008, 12)

This 'family practices' approach to understanding families is the first step towards rethinking childhood and families. The advantage of the 'family practices' approach is that it moves us way from rigid and static stances on childhood, which, as we saw with the work of Patricia Morgan earlier, tends to privilege certain forms of the family, and by implications disadvantages children who live in 'non-traditional' family settings.

The childhood experience of family is indeed diverse – families can be a site of comfort, care and love or a place of abuse, violence and dislike. These relationships, whether caring or abusive, are always underpinned by power and power relationships. So if we are to rethink children and families we need to think about power and how it is deployed.

In this book we have explored two potentially powerful concepts that can contribute to change in the deployment of power: they are 'authoritative parenting' and the 'democratic family', which were explored in Chapter 3.

The role of the parent is central to the concerns of this book. Parenting has a major impact on us all – it is a key influence on our personalities, our social capital and on our live chances. In this book we have explored different styles of parenting and suggested that authoritative parenting is the most progressive of the models analysed. Authoritative parenting was earlier identified as having the following features:

> They [authoritative parents] want their children to be assertive as well as socially responsible and self-regulated as well as cooperative. (Baumrind, 1991, 62)

The delicate balance of parenting is to offer a balance of provision, protection and participation, to utilize the language of children's rights. This is a complex package where slipping into too much or too little of one of these categories can have a major impact on the child. For example, too much protection can limit the autonomy of the child.

The authoritative parent is aware of how to deploy a balance of the three key elements – protection, participation and provision. Where this is carried out with respect for the child, and in full consultation with the child, parenting will be effective and supportive.

The role of the State is to step in when these elements of parenting are not delivered effectively, particularly when there is what we have previously identified as 'low warmth/high criticism' parenting. The State should, where children are not at risk of 'significant harm', offer support to parents in attempting to develop more authoritative parenting styles. Where a child is at risk of 'significant harm' the State should consider a more protective approach to children, while simultaneously ensuring that it maximizes participation by children. As Linda Gordon's work, outlined in Chapter 2, made clear high quality professional work can make real improvements for children, and empower them in taking more control over their own lives.

Rethinking children and the State

Just as power is fundamental in understanding children and families, so is it essential to understanding the relationship between childhood and the State. In most States – be they liberal democratic or more authoritarian – the power flow is mainly unidirectional, it flows from the State and attempts to regulate childhood. In order to rethink the relationship between childhood and the State we need to contribute to changing the singular direction of the flow of power.

It is argued here that many commentators misread the modern liberal states' current attitude to participation by children. For example, Hendrick argues that the British New Labour government (1997–2010) viewed children as

> too valuable in terms of human capital to be given any say in shaping their own lives. (Hendrick, 2003, 253)

This is actually to misread the situation where children's participation has been actively promoted as part of the Every Child Matters programme (2003–2010) in England and other governments internationally (see Jones, 2009, 149). Government policy in England, for example, demands that agencies

> Involve children and young people in this process, and when inspectors assess how local areas are doing they will listen especially to the views of children and young people. (www.everychildmatters.gov.uk/aims – viewed 3 February 2010)

In each local authority in England the Children's Trusts have responsibilities to ensure the active participation of children in informing and influencing policy.

Research is showing the ways in which local authorities are encouraging the active participation of children in informing and influencing policy (Combe, 2002). A specific example of this, relating to children in care, was seen in 2008 in the Children and Young Person's Act which required each local authority to have a children in care committee where children are actively consulted. Thus the approach taken by Stein accurately sums up the current situation:

> Today, we take it for granted that policy makers and practitioners should listen to the views of young people living in, and leaving, care. But this has not always been so. We owe a lot to the activities of the Who Cares? project in the 1970s, the National Association of Young People in Care in the 1980s and 1990s, and, currently, to A National Voice, for bringing about important changes in the way young people in care are involved in decisions that affect their lives. (Rainer, 2007, 4)

While Stein is referring to children in care his quote has a wider resonance. He reflects on how children participate more fully than before, but he also reflects on how, in this particular example, this has been brought about by children organizing for their rights, sometimes in partnership with supportive adults.

We can argue therefore that an effective participation model requires both a proactive stance by supportive adults and children campaigning and organizing autonomously.

The State requires multiple points of engagement with children. It needs to engage with children in general, through active support for universal organizations such as youth councils and children's parliaments. The State also needs to engage with children where they are part of specific groups – such as children in care, disabled children or children from particular ethnic groups, for example.

The charity Action for Children utilizes the idea of a 'child-fair State' to explain how the State can remodel the way it relates to children. Their policy is outlined in the box below.

A child-fair State

Action for Children calls for a child-fair state, that actively promotes a positive vision for children and young people as full citizens. Children cannot be used as political footballs, and moral panics and headlines must not be allowed to take precedence over their needs.

Action for Children demands a political system that puts the long-term needs of children first and short-term politics second. We call on all the main political parties of the United Kingdom to give children the commitment they need, for as long as it takes.

1. In all four nations of the United Kingdom, the Children's Minister must be in a permanent Cabinet/Executive-level position to represent and speak on behalf of children and hold all parts of government to account.
2. Before the next general election, a cross-party group must establish a 21-year vision for children and young people that all the main parties must sign up to. Then, at the beginning of every new government, the cross-party group must set out or reaffirm its vision, which is binding on all parties.
3. Any new initiative for children and young people must be funded for at least six years, with exceptions to be granted only by agreement with the Children's Minister.
4. Every government department and agency across the United Kingdom must examine how its policies impact on children and young people, and report annually on this to Parliaments and Assemblies.
5. All UK media bodies and organizations with governance of media, including Ofcom, the Advertising Standards Authority and the Press Complaints Commission, must establish a consultation committee made up of children and young people.

Action for Children (2008) *As Long as It Takes: A New Politics for Children*. London: Action for Children

This manifesto contains the seeds of a new compact between the State and childhood. By working along the lines suggested here, by developing the approaches suggested in the United Nations Charter for the Rights of Children and the work of Children's Commissioners across the world, we will be moving towards a more child-fair world.

A model for participation

The research examples and theoretical discussions in this book have pointed us in a particular direction. In much of the research where children have spoken about their perspectives they have asked for adults to carry out adult responsibilities in a child-centred manner, but they have not wanted to totally control decision-making. This is reflected in many of the research studies explored in this book. For example, Butler, et al.'s (pp. 86–7 above) work on decision-making showed how children valued having a voice, but did not expect their views to be finally determinative. Equally the work of Drakeford et al. (pp. 69–70 above) demonstrates how children want to participate, how they have strong views on particular issues, but do not wish to be responsible for wide-ranging policy decision-making. This research suggests that we need to locate children's participation appropriately. Berry Mayall and Mike Stein below make suggestions as to how this might work in practice.

First, policy and practice needs to be informed by what Mayall identifies as a child standpoint:

> Including young people's knowledge in intersection with adult knowledge is essential in three major tasks. It is an essential journey of discovery: to provide a coherent account of how a constituent social group of the population experience and understand their social positioning. It is essential for working towards a comprehensive account of how the social order works, and in particular the degree of fit between these valuable strangers' experience and the relations of ruling. And it is essential as a first step towards shifting how adults think about adult-child relations, and towards taking account of young peoples experience and knowledge in re-shaping the social order. On all counts it is a political enterprise. (2002, 139)

Stein suggests how complex and nuanced this process is:

> Achieving effective participation remains an ongoing challenge. It requires a clear conceptualisation of participation recognising the different levels of power, the different forms of consultation, the different groups of children and young

people, the distinction between decision relating to individual and groups, and between private and public domains. Further complexities include interpreting what children and young people are saying, the status of their views within the wider policy process, and the impact of their views – the outcomes of their participation. (2006b, 180)

The research suggests that children want to be consulted, want to participate and that they want a voice. They also want to work with what Action for Children might call 'child fair' adults, adopting a 'child standpoint', who have a strong focus on ensuring that the voice of children is heard and acted upon.

What all of the approaches discussed above have in common is attempting to reduce and change the flow of power outlined in Figure 1.1. In summary the democratic family, authoritative parenting, a child-centred, 'child fair' State taking into account a 'child standpoint', and fully encouraging children's participation at all levels will all contribute to empowering children.

The children's workforce will have a crucial role to play in changing and rethinking childhood. All professionals working with children can help reduce to flow of power over children by adopting some of the approaches taken in this book.

Activities

The following activities are designed to help reflect back on some of the key concerns over the book as a whole.

Activity 1

Choose an example of professional work with children. Assess the following questions:

> How are children involved in influencing policy and practice in that work?
> How could that involvement be enhanced or developed?

Activity 2

Choose an example of a household you know well, perhaps the one you live in. Assess the following questions:

> How are children involved in influencing the daily life of that household?
> How could that involvement be enhanced or developed?

Summary

This chapter has

Asked how can we reinvent the relationship between children and families?
Asked how can we reinvent the relationship between children and the State?
Suggested that the democratic family, authoritarian parenting and a 'child-fair' State can help transform the control of children over their own lives
Argued that the task of parents, carers and professionals is to do what they can to reverse the flow of power so that children have more power over their own lives

Further reading

Jones, P. (2009) *Rethinking Childhood: Attitudes in Contemporary Society*. London: Continuum.

The first book in this series which provides a comprehensive overview of contemporary research about children and how this can be utilized to reinvent the experience of childhood.

Mayall, B. (2002) *Towards a Sociology for Childhood*. Buckingham: Open University Press.

This book provides a sociology of childhood, builds on, and is illustrated by, direct research work exploring the everyday lives of children. Mayall makes suggestions about how childhood can be reinvented and rethought.

References

11 Million (2008) *Claiming Asylum at a Screening Unit as an Unaccompanied Child.* London: 11 Million

Action for Children (2008) *As Long as It Takes: A New Politics for Children.* London: Action for Children

Ariès, P. (1979) *Centuries of Childhood.* Harmondsworth: Peregrine

Barnardo's (2008) *The Shame of Britain's Intolerance to Children,* Barkingside: Barnardo's

Bauman, Z. (2003) *Wasted Lives, Modernity and Its Outcasts.* Cambridge: Polity

Bauman, Z. (2007) *Liquid Love.* Cambridge: Polity

Baumrind, D. (1991) 'The influence of parenting style on adolescent competence and substance use', *Journal of Early Adolescence,* 11, (1), 56–95

Bean, P. and Melville, J. (1990) *Lost Children of the Empire.* London: Unwin Hyman, pp 38–60

Beck Gernsheim, E. (2002) *Reinventing the Family.* Cambridge: Polity

Berger, B. and Berger, P. (1983) *The War Over the Family: Capturing the Middle Ground.* Harmondsworth: Penguin

Bradshaw, J. (2002) *The Well-being of Children in the United Kingdom.* London: Save the Children

Bronfenbrenner, U. (1974) *Two Worlds of Childhood.* Harmondsworth: Penguin

Butler, I., Robinson, M. and Scanlan, L. (2005) *Children and Decision-Making.* National Children's Bureau: London

Butler-Sloss, E. (1988) *Report of the Inquiry into Child Abuse in Cleveland 1987.* London: HMSO

Cabinet Office/Department of Children, Schools and Families, (2008), *Families in Britain: An Evidence Paper.* London

Campbell, B. (1988) *Unofficial Secrets – Child Sexual Abuse: The Cleveland Case.* London: Virago

Cohen, S. (1973) *Folk Devils and Moral Panics.* London: Paladin

Coontz, S. (2000) 'Historical perspectives on family studies', *Journal of Marriage and the Family,* (US) 62, 283–297

Cunningham, H. (1995) *Children and Childhood in Western Society since 1500.* London: Longman

Darling, N. (1999) 'Parenting style and its correlates', *ERIC Digest.* EDO-PS-99-3

Dencik, L. (1989) 'Growing up in the Postmodern age', *Acta Sociologica,* 32, (2), 155–180

De Mause, L. (ed.) (1976) *The History of Childhood.* London: Souvenir Press

Department for Children, Schools and Families (2007) *The Children's Plan: Building Brighter Futures.* London: Stationery Office.

Department for Education and Skills (2003) *Every Child Matters.* London: DfES

Department of Health (1995) *Child Protection: Messages from Research.* London: HMSO, p. 158

Donzelot, J. (1979) *The Policing of Families: Welfare versus the State.* London: Hutchinson

Drakeford, M., Scourfield, J., Holland, S. and Davies, A. (2009) 'Welsh Children's Views on Government and Participation', *Childhood* 16, 247–264

Edwards, B. (1974) *The Burston School Strike*. London: Lawrence and Wishart

Ennew, J. (1986) *The Sexual Exploitation of Children*. Cambridge: Polity

Etzioni, A. (1993) *The Spirit of Community: Rights, Responsibilities and the Communitarian Agenda*. New York: Simon and Schuster.

Finkelhor, D. (1986) *A Sourcebook on Child Sexual Abuse*. Newbury Park: Sage

Frost, N. (2005) *Joined-up Thinking, Partnership and Professionalism*. Dartington: Research in Practice

Frost, N., Mills, S. and Stein, M. (1999) *Understanding Residential Care*. Aldershot: Ashgate

Frost, N. and Parton, N. (2009) *Understanding Children's Social Care*. London: Sage

Garrett, P. M. (2009) *'Transforming' Children's Services*. London, McGraw Hill

Giddens, A. (1999) *Runaway World*. London: Profile Books

Glisson, C. and Hemmelgarn, A. (2003) 'The effects of organisational climate and inter-organizational coordination on the quality and outcomes of children's service systems', *Child Abuse and Neglect*, 22, (5), 401–421

Gordon, L. (1986) *Heroes of Their Own Lives: the Politics and History of Family Violence*. London: Virago

Gordon, L (1989) *Heroes of Their Own Lives: The Politics and History of Family Violence*. London: Virago

Hek, R. (2005) *The Experiences and Needs of Refugee and Asylum Seeking Children in the UK: A Literature Review*. Birmingham: University of Birmingham.

Hendrick, H. (1994) *Child Welfare: England 1872–1989*. London: Routledge

Hendrick, H. (2003) *Child Welfare*. Bristol: Policy Press

Hindess, B. (1973) *The Use of Official Statistics: A Critique of Positivism and Ethno-methodology*. London: MacMillan

Hirsch, D., and Smith, N. (2010) 'Family values – parents' views on necessities for families with children', *Research Report 641*. London: Department for Work and Families

Holland, S. and O'Neill, S. (2006) '"We had to be there to make sure it was what we wanted": enabling children's participation in family decision-making through the family group conference', *Childhood*, 13, (1) 91–111

Holt, J. (1975) *Escape from Childhood*. Harmondsworth: Pelican

Illich, I. (1973) *De-schooling Society*. Harmondsworth: Penguin

James, A., Jenks, C. and Prout, A. (1998) *Theorising Childhood*. Cambridge: Polity Press

Jenks, C. (1996) *Childhood*. London: Routledge

Jones, P. (2009) *Rethinking Childhood: Attitudes in Contemporary Society*. London: Continuum

Laming, H. (2003) *The Victoria Climbié Report: Report of an Inquiry by Lord Laming*. London: The Stationery Office

Leeson, C. (2007) 'My life in care: experiences of non-participation in decision-making processes in decision-making processes', *Child & Family Social Work*, 12, (3), 268–277

Mason, J. and Tipper, B. (2008) 'Being Related: How Children Define and Create Kinship', *Childhood*, 15, (4), 441–460

Mayall, B. (2002) *Towards a Sociology for Childhood*. Buckingham: Open University Press

McGrew, A. (1992) 'The State in advanced capitalist States', in J. Allen, P. Braham and P. Lewis (eds) *Political and Economic Forms of Modernity*. Cambridge: Polity, 65–216

Mitchell, F. (2007) 'Assessment practice with unaccompanied children: exploring exceptions to the problem', in Morgan, R. (2006) *About Social Workers: A Children's View Report*. London: CSCI.

Morgan, P. (1998) 'An endangered species?' in M. David (ed.) *The Fragmented Family: Does It Matter?* London: Institute for Economic Affairs, 64–82

Parton, N. (1985) *The Politics of Child Abuse*. Basingstoke: Macmillan.

Parton, N. (1991) *Governing the Family: Child Care, Child Protection and the State*. Basingstoke: Macmillan.

Parton, N. (2006) *Safeguarding Childhood*. London: Palgrave

Parton, N. and O'Byrne, P. (2000) *Constructive Social Work: Towards a New Practice*. Basingstoke: MacMillan

Pearson, G. (1983) *Hooligan: A History of Respectable Fears*. Basingstoke: Palgrave

Piaget, J. (1959) *The Language and Thought of the Child*. London: Routledge

Pollock, L. (1983) *Forgotten Children: Parent-Child Relations*. Cambridge: Cambridge University Press

Postman, N. (1994) *The Disappearance of Childhood*. New York: Vintage

Qvurtup, J. (2005) *Studies in Modern Childhood*. London: Palgrave

Riley, D. (1983) *War in the Nursery: Theories of the Child and Mother*. London: Virago

Rothwell, A (2008)

Feral Children: what is Barnardo's playing at? www.intelligentgiving.com

Scruton, P. (ed.) (1997) *Childhood in Crisis*. London: UCL Press

Smart, C. (2007) *Personal Life*. Cambridge: Polity

Smith, R. (2010) *A Universal Child?* Basingstoke: Palgrave

Stein, M. (2006b) 'A Wrong Turn?' *Guardian*, 6.1.2006

Stein. M. (2009) *Quality Protects*. London: Jessica Kingsley Press

UNHCHR (2008) *Committee on the Rights of the Child – 49ᵗʰ Session*. Geneva: UNHCHR

UNICEF (2007) 'Child poverty in perspective: an overview of child well-being in Rich Countries', *Innocenti Report Card no.7*. Florence

Valentine, G. (1996) 'Angels and devils: moral landscapes of childhood', *Society and Space*, 14, 581–599.

Wardhaugh, J. and Wilding, P. (1993) 'Towards an explanation of the corruption of care', *Critical Social Policy*, 37, 4–31

Warner, M. (1989) *Into the Dangerous World: Some Thoughts on Childhood and Its Costs*. London: Counterblast

Waterhouse, R. (2000) *Lost in Care: Summary of Report*. London: Stationery Office

Williams, F. (2004) *Rethinking Families*. London: Calouste Gulbenkian Foundation

Young, S. (2008) 'Indigenous child protection policy in Australia: Using whiteness theory for social work', *Sites*, 5, (1), 102–123

Zhou, X. and Hou, L. (1999) 'Children of the cultural revolution: the State and the life course in the People's Republic of China', *American Sociological Review*, 64, (1), 12–36

Index